THIS COLORING BOOK BELONGS TO:

I0491157

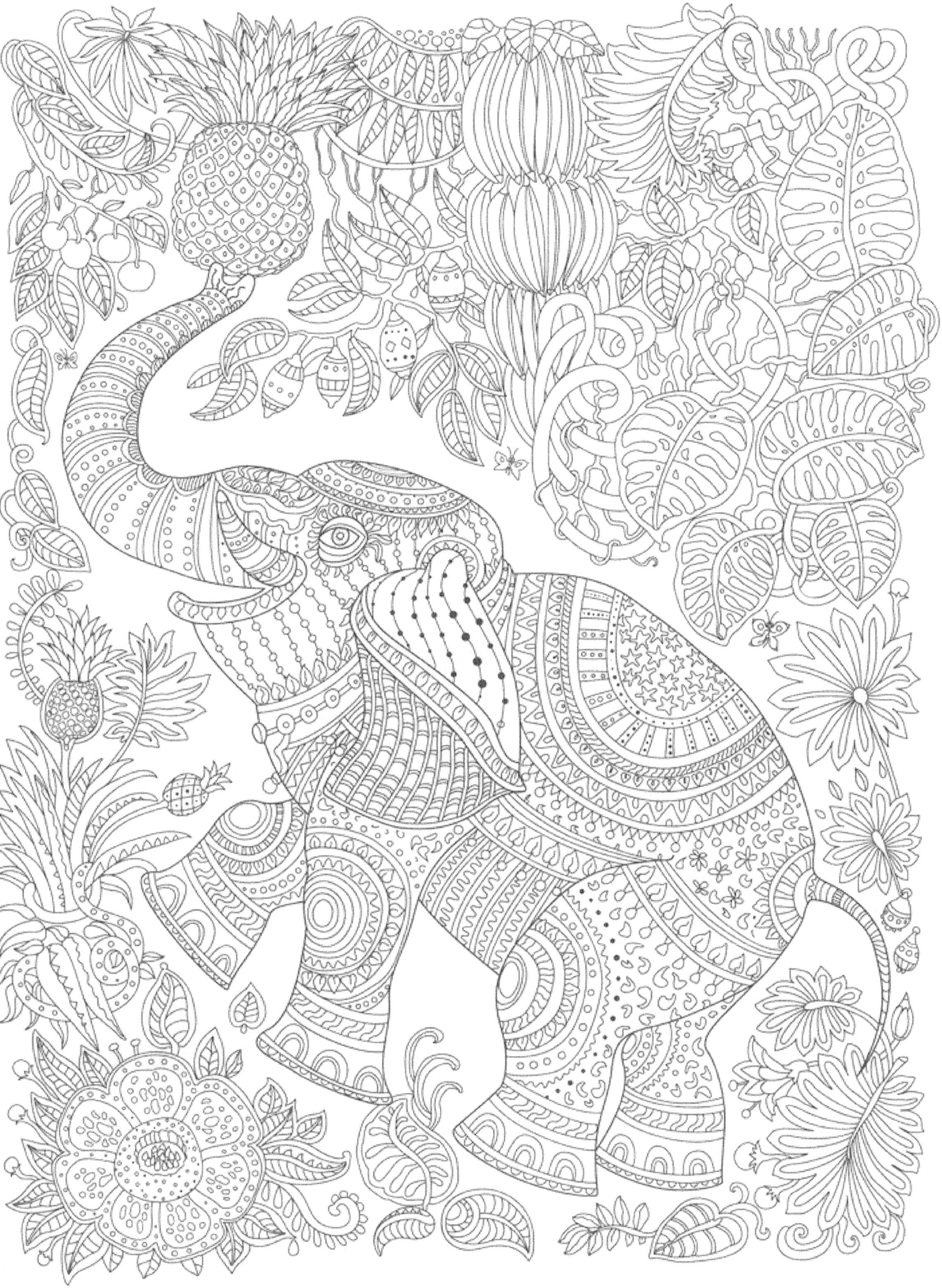

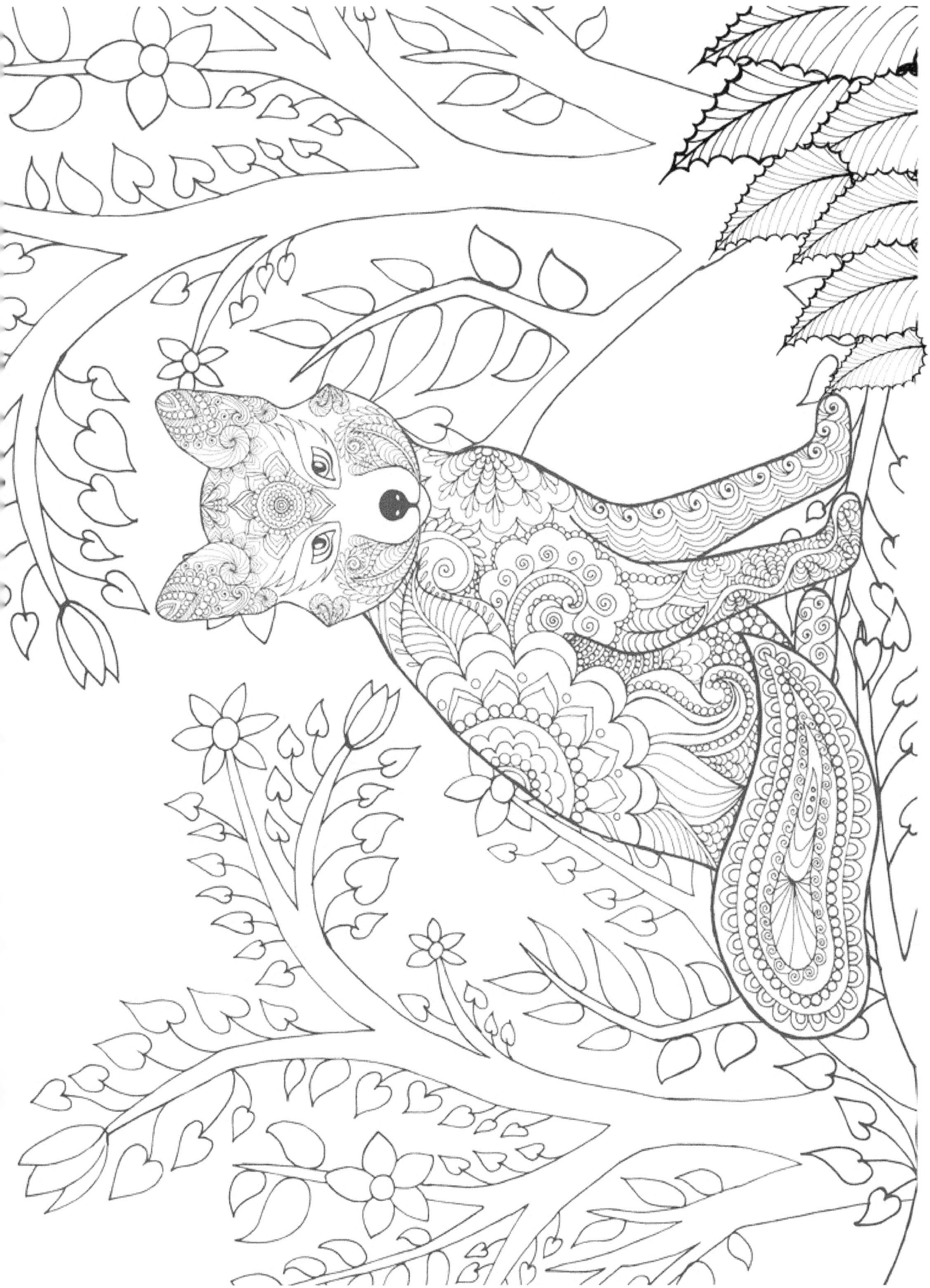

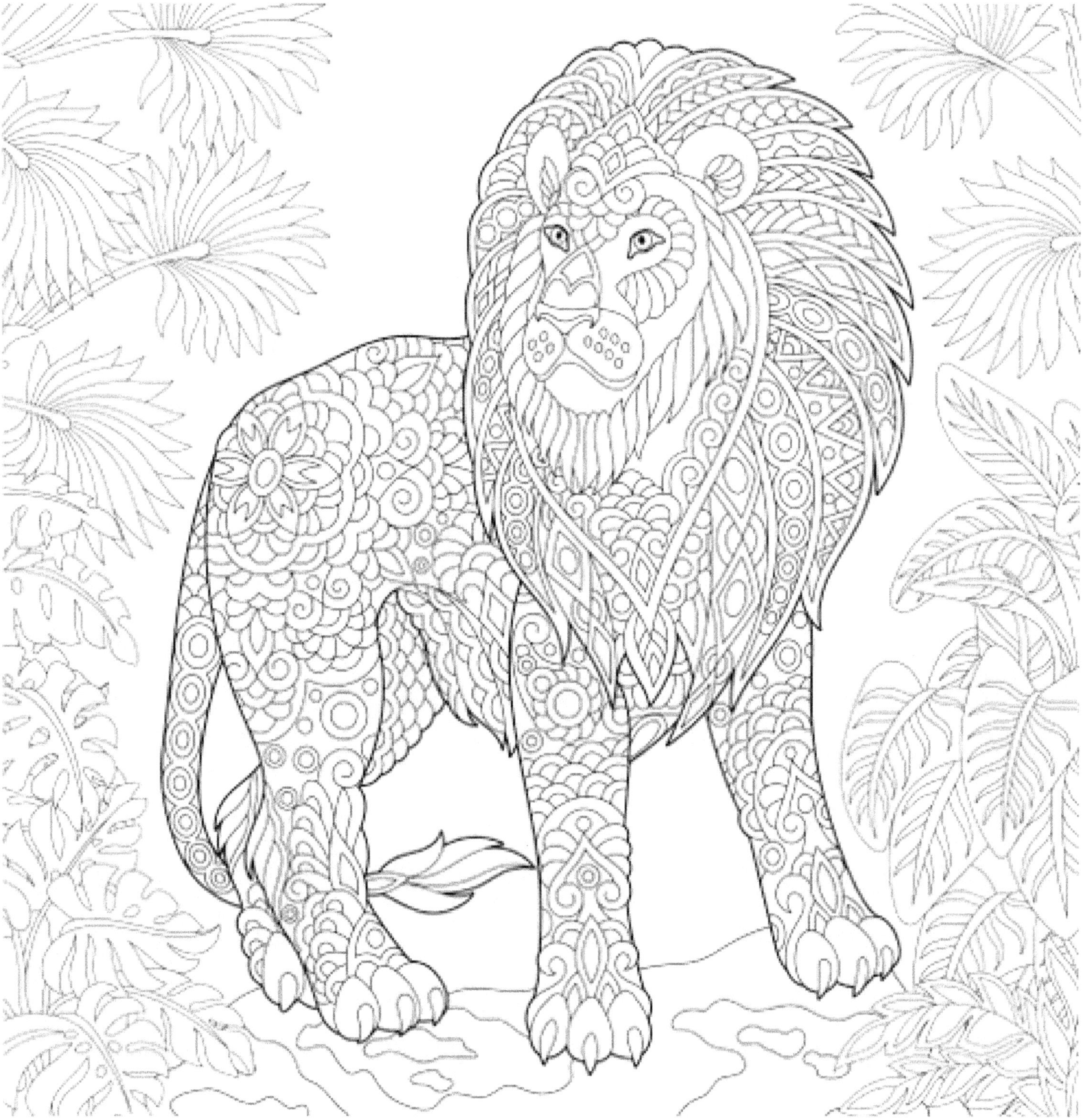

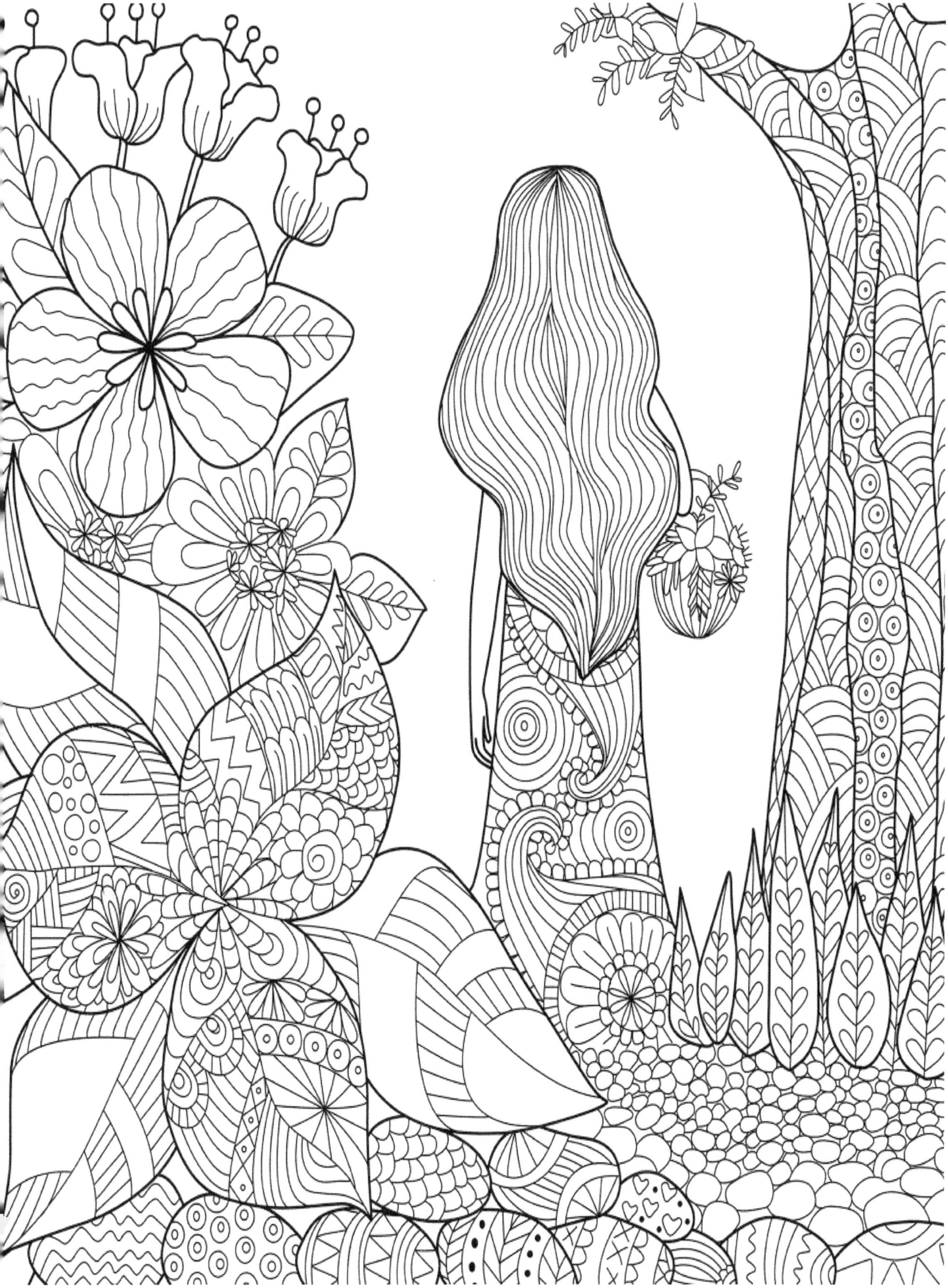

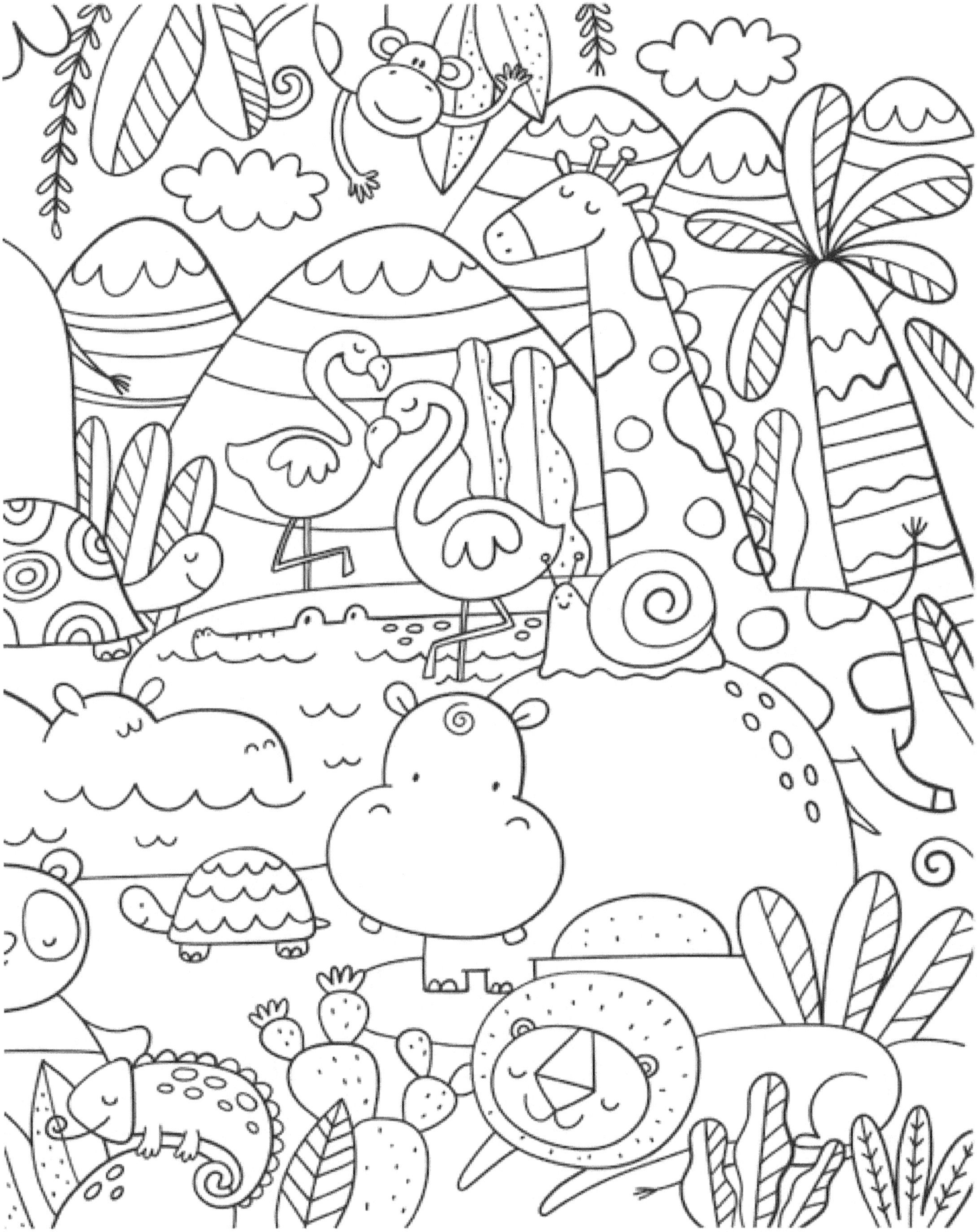

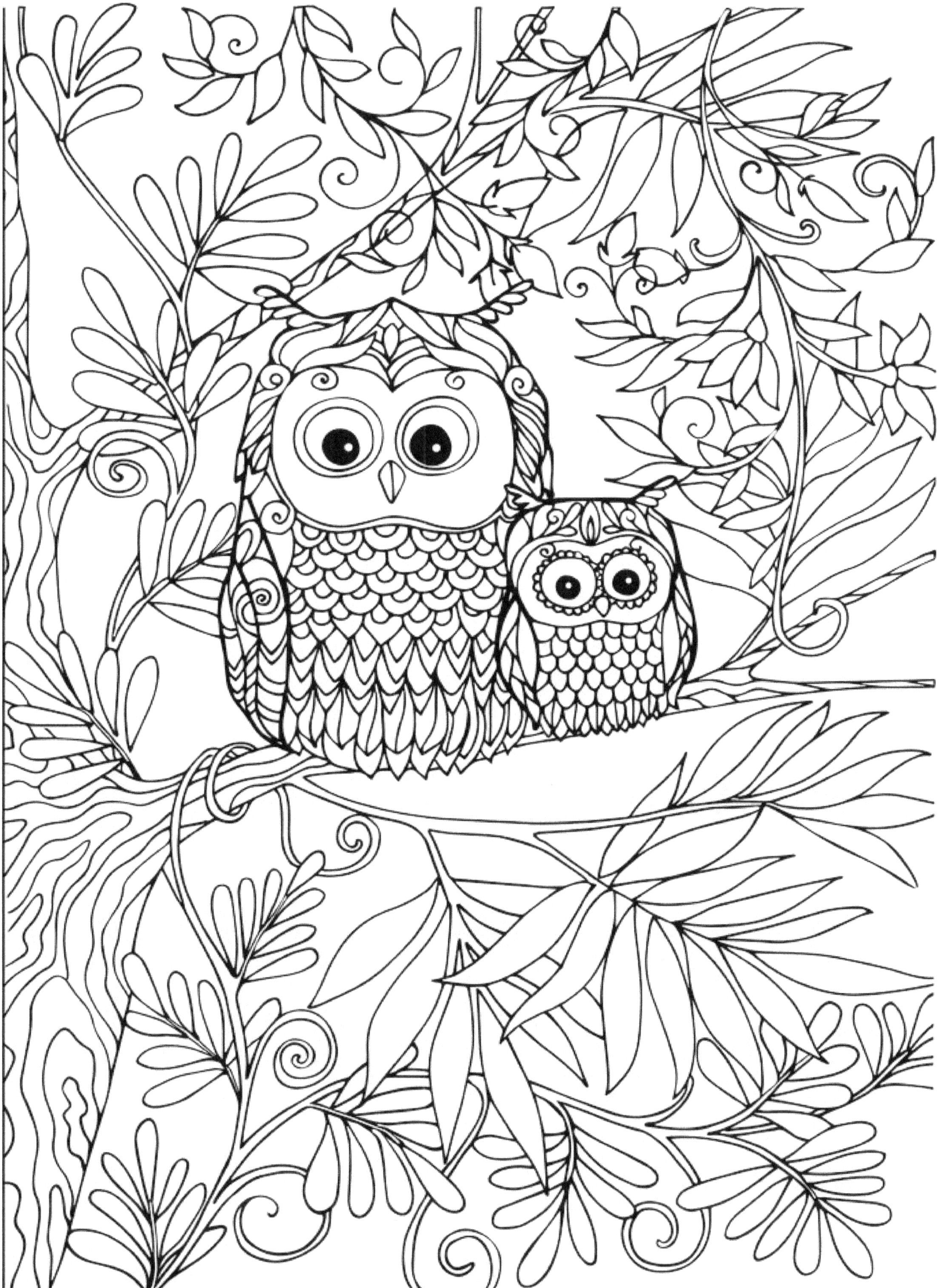

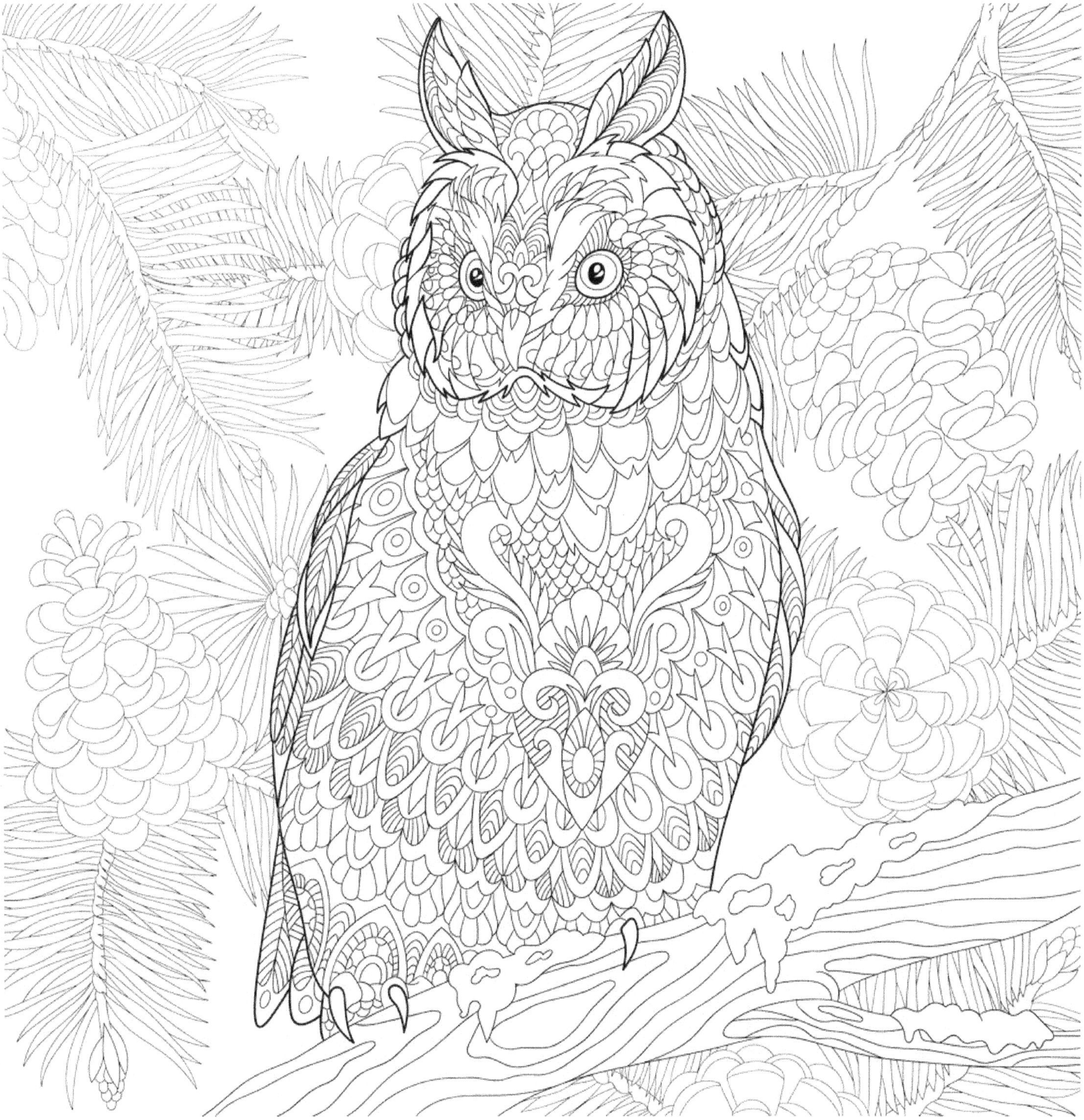

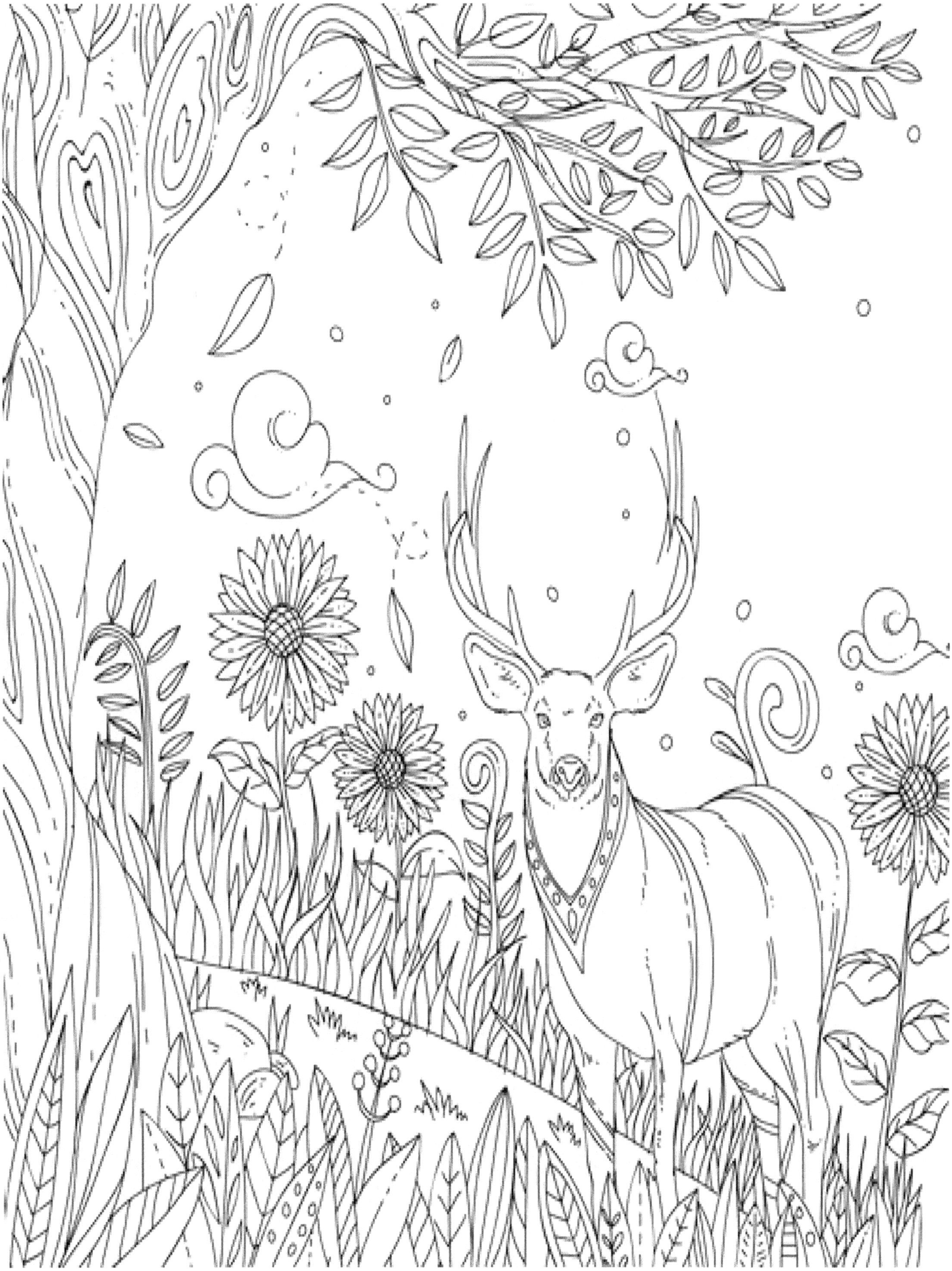

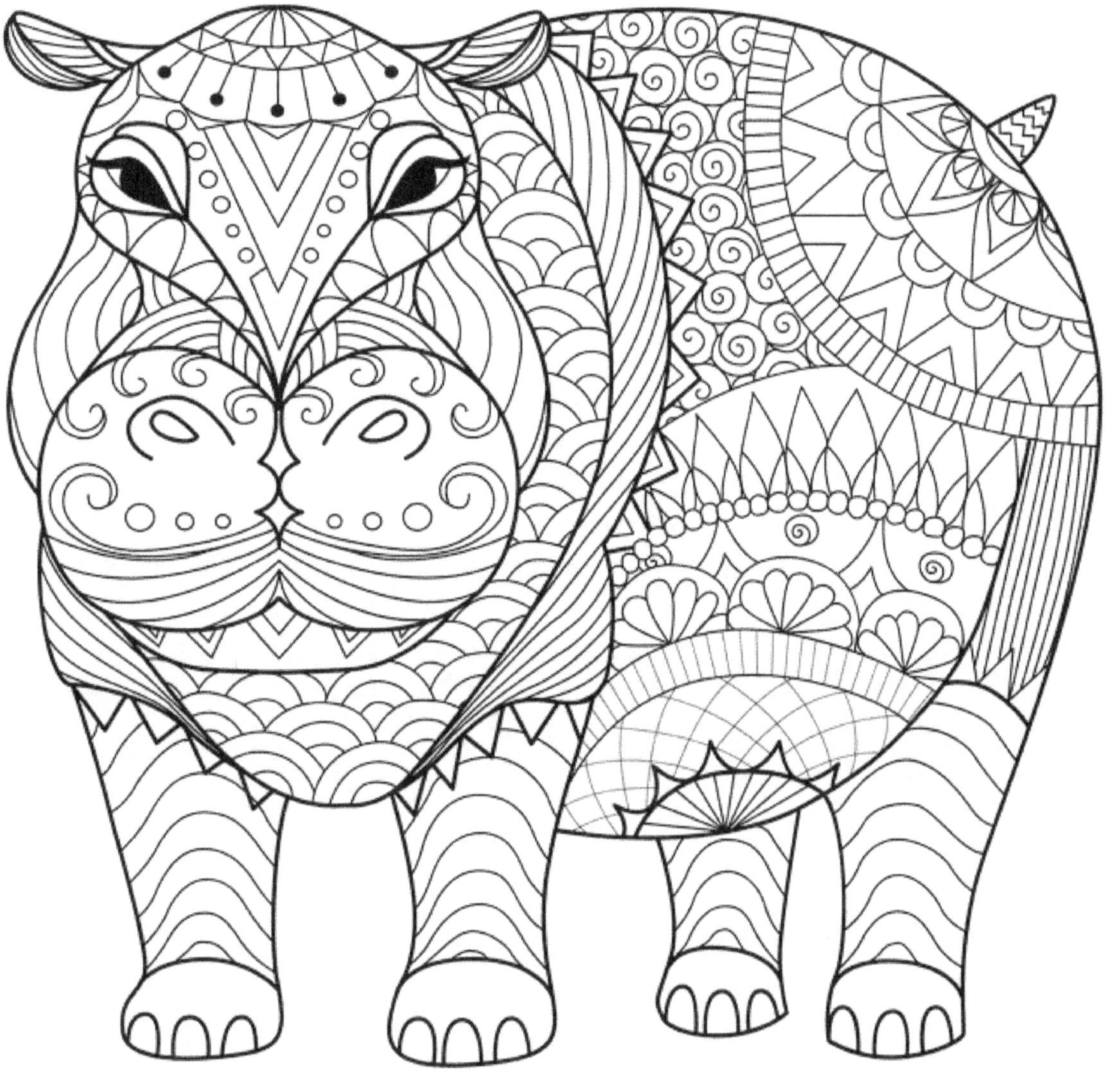

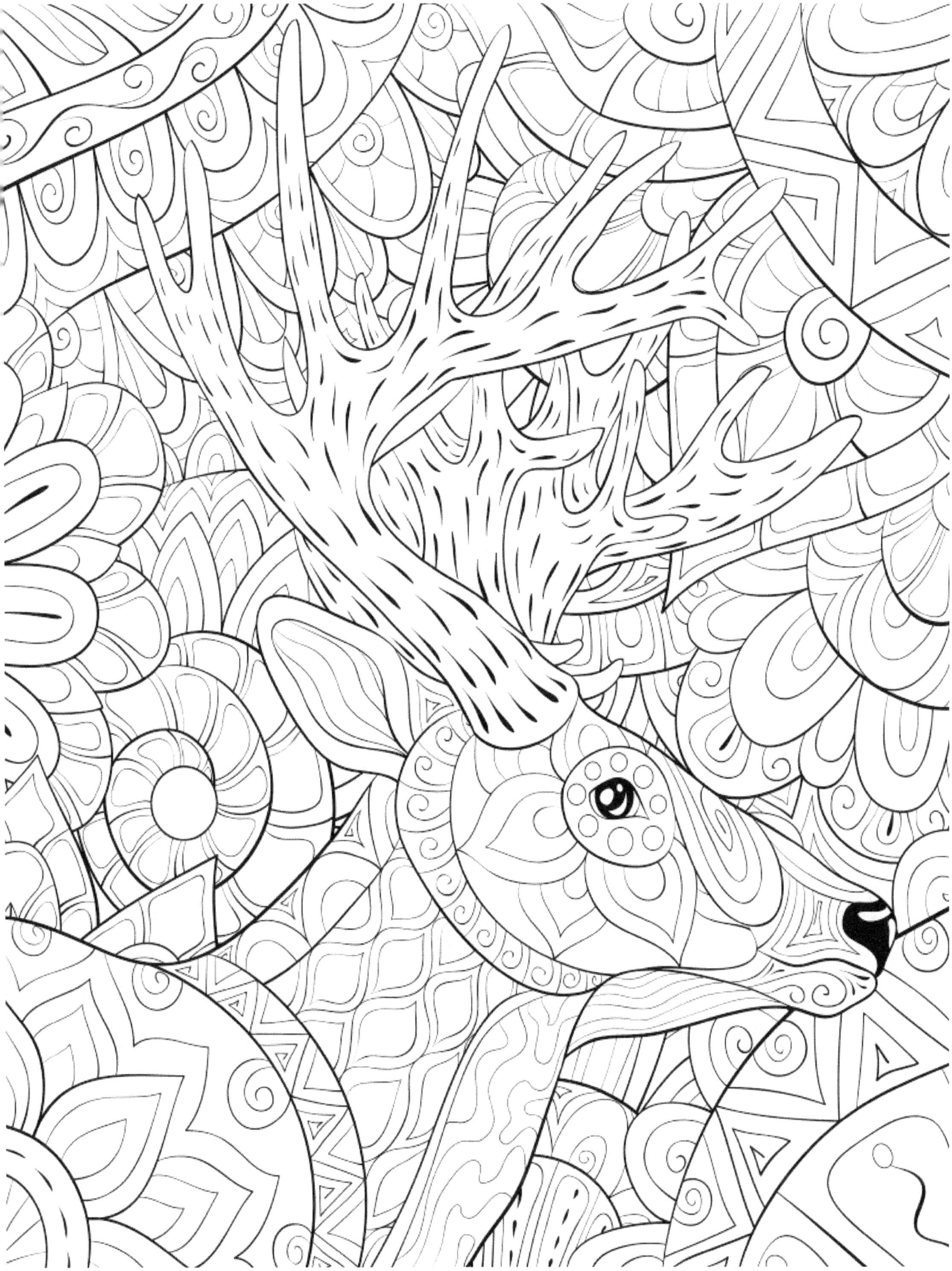

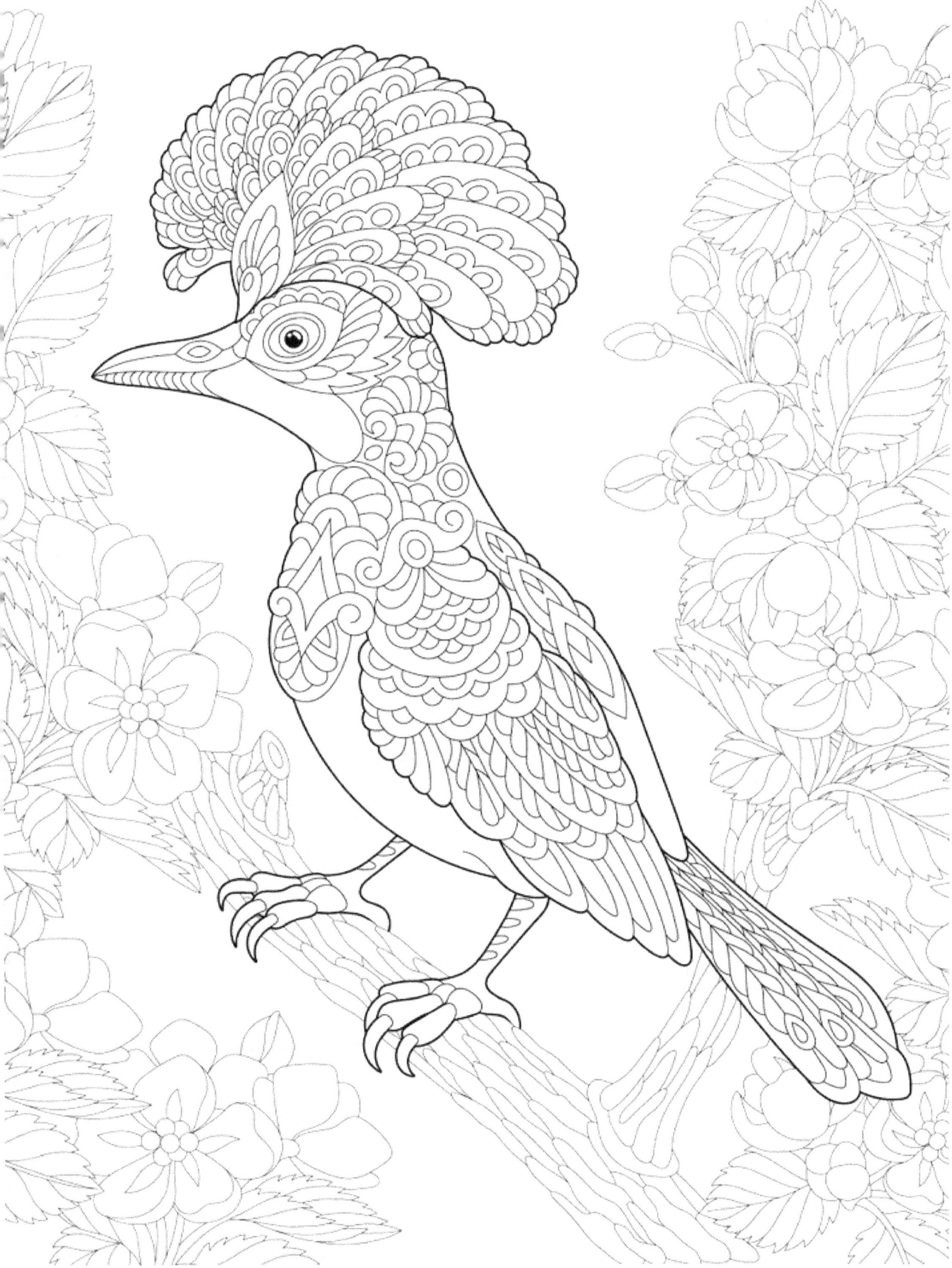

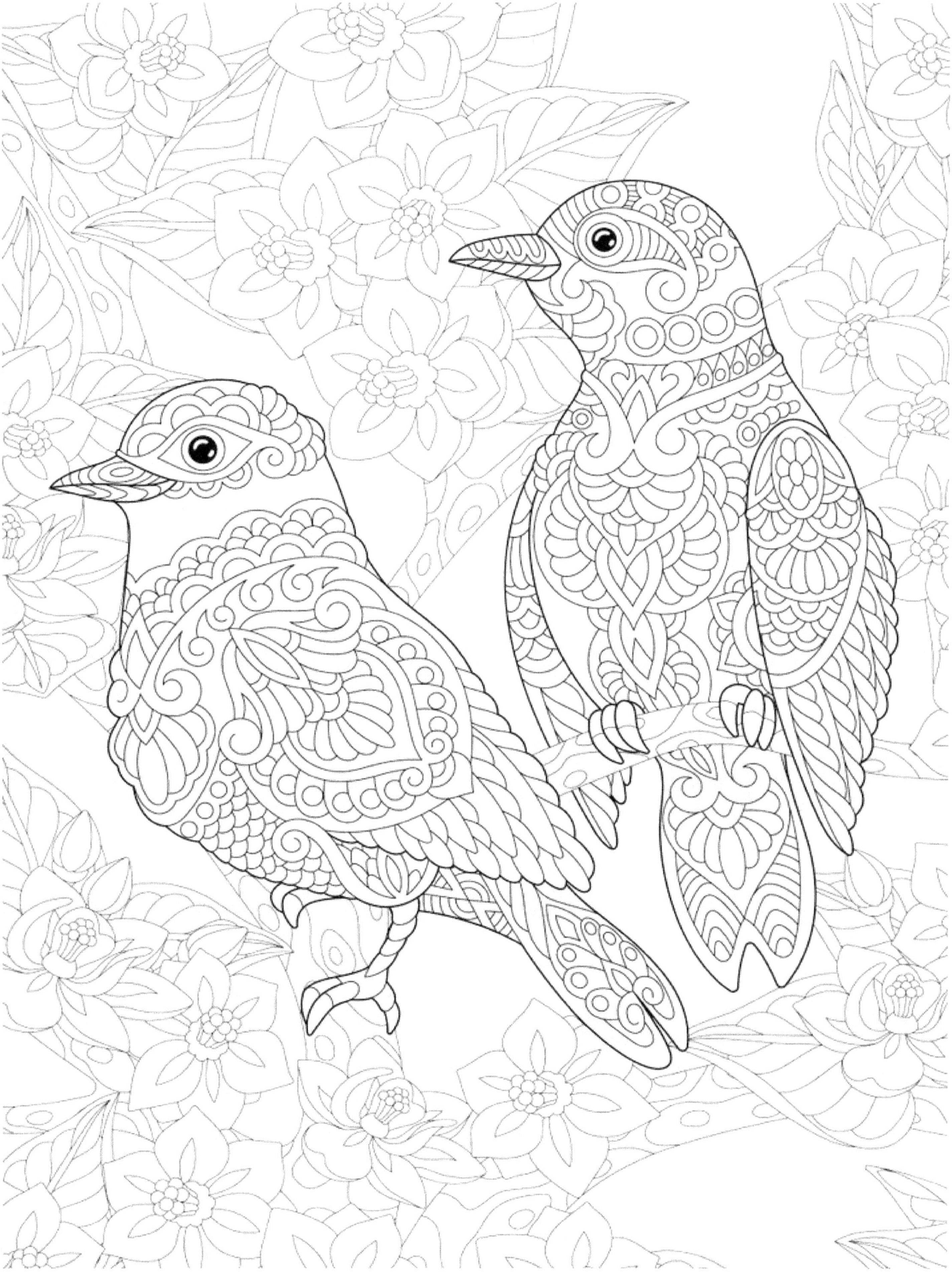

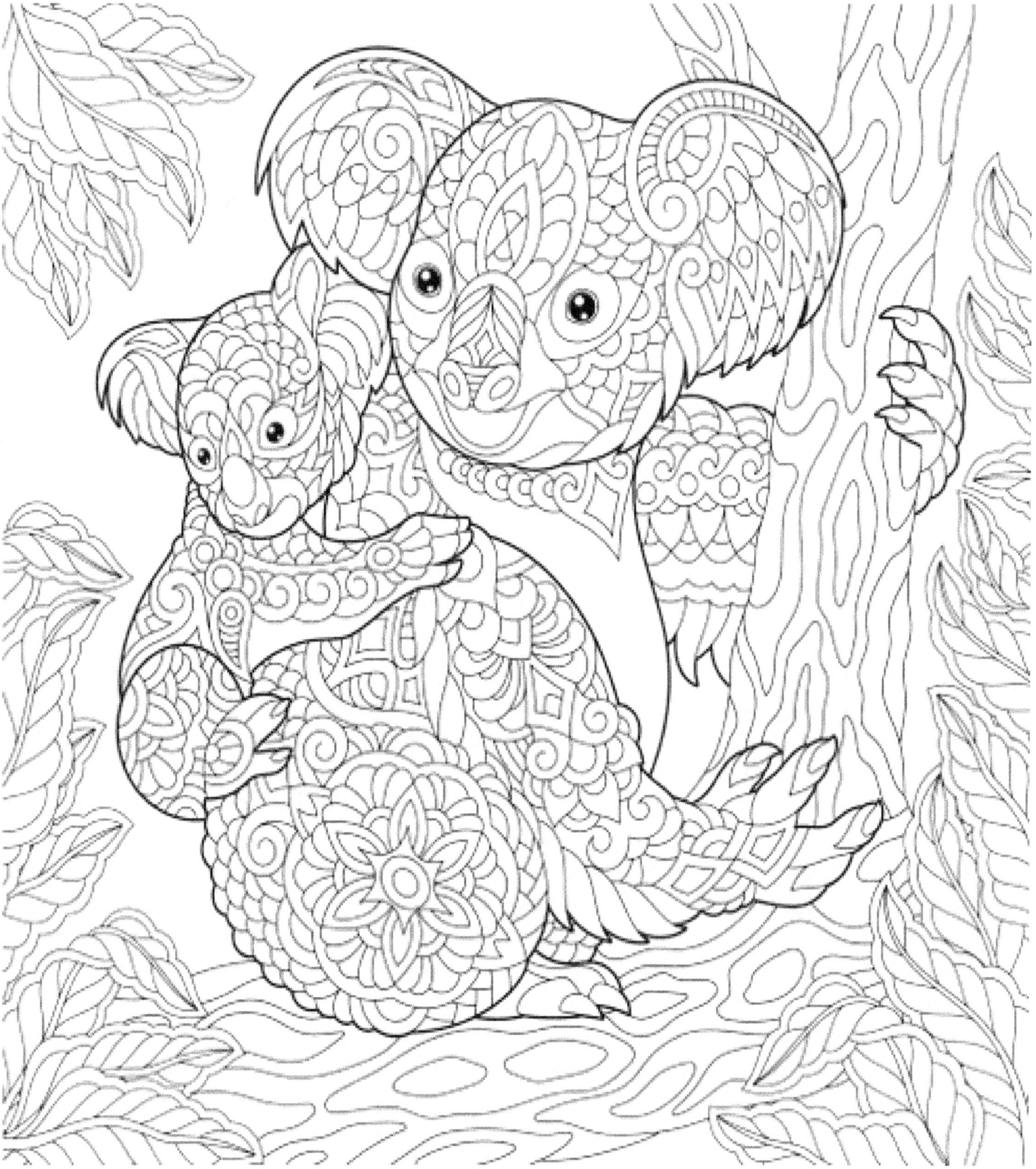

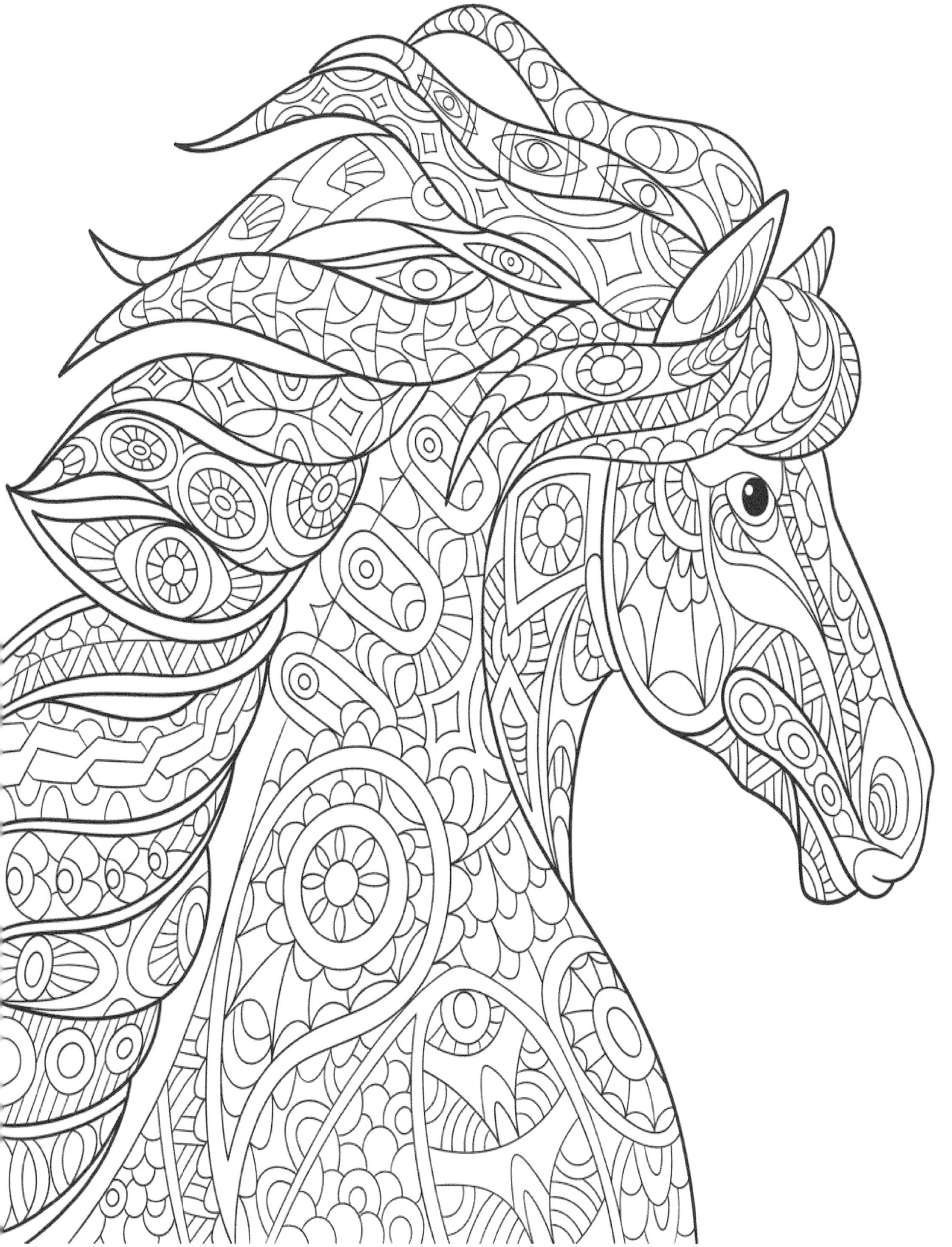

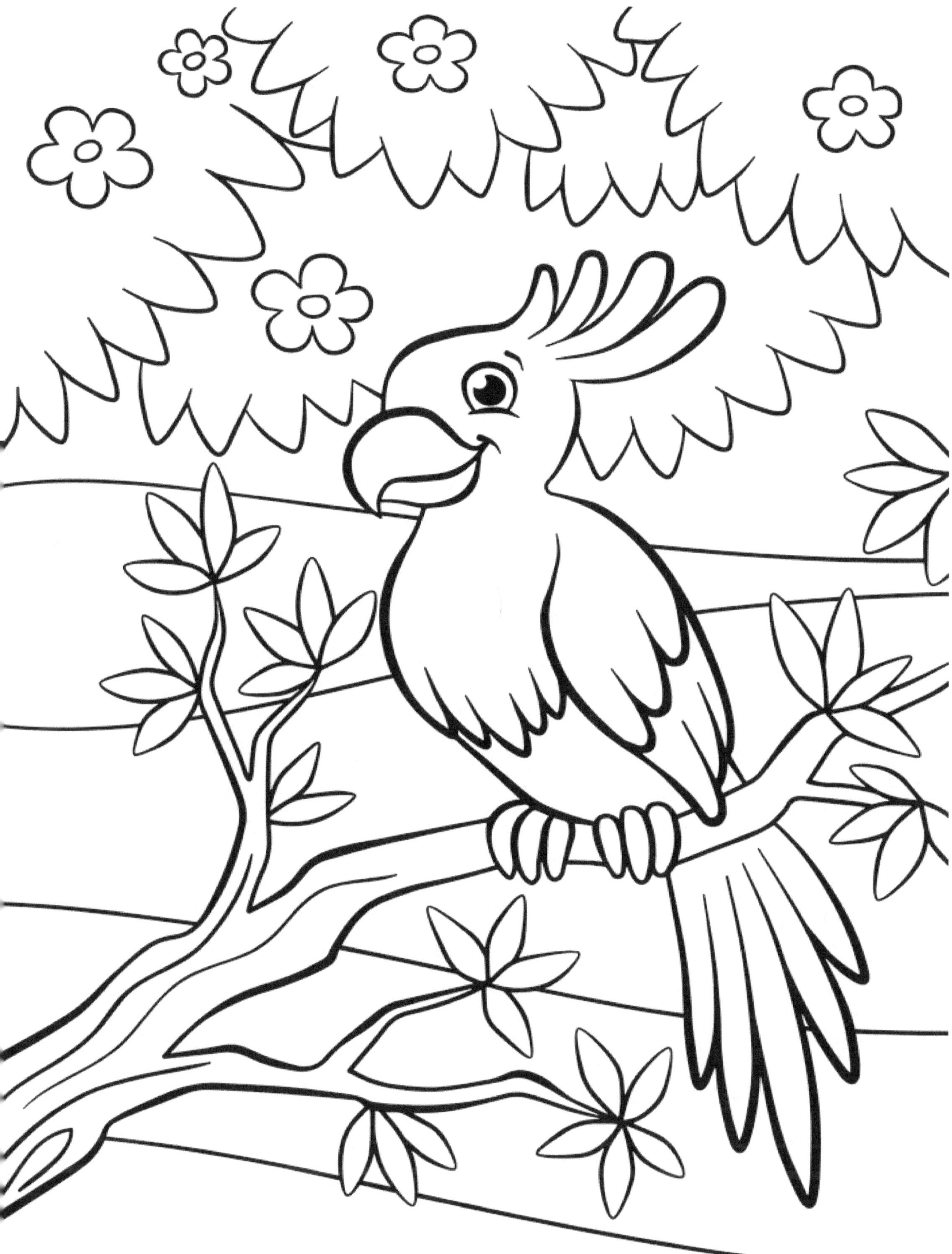

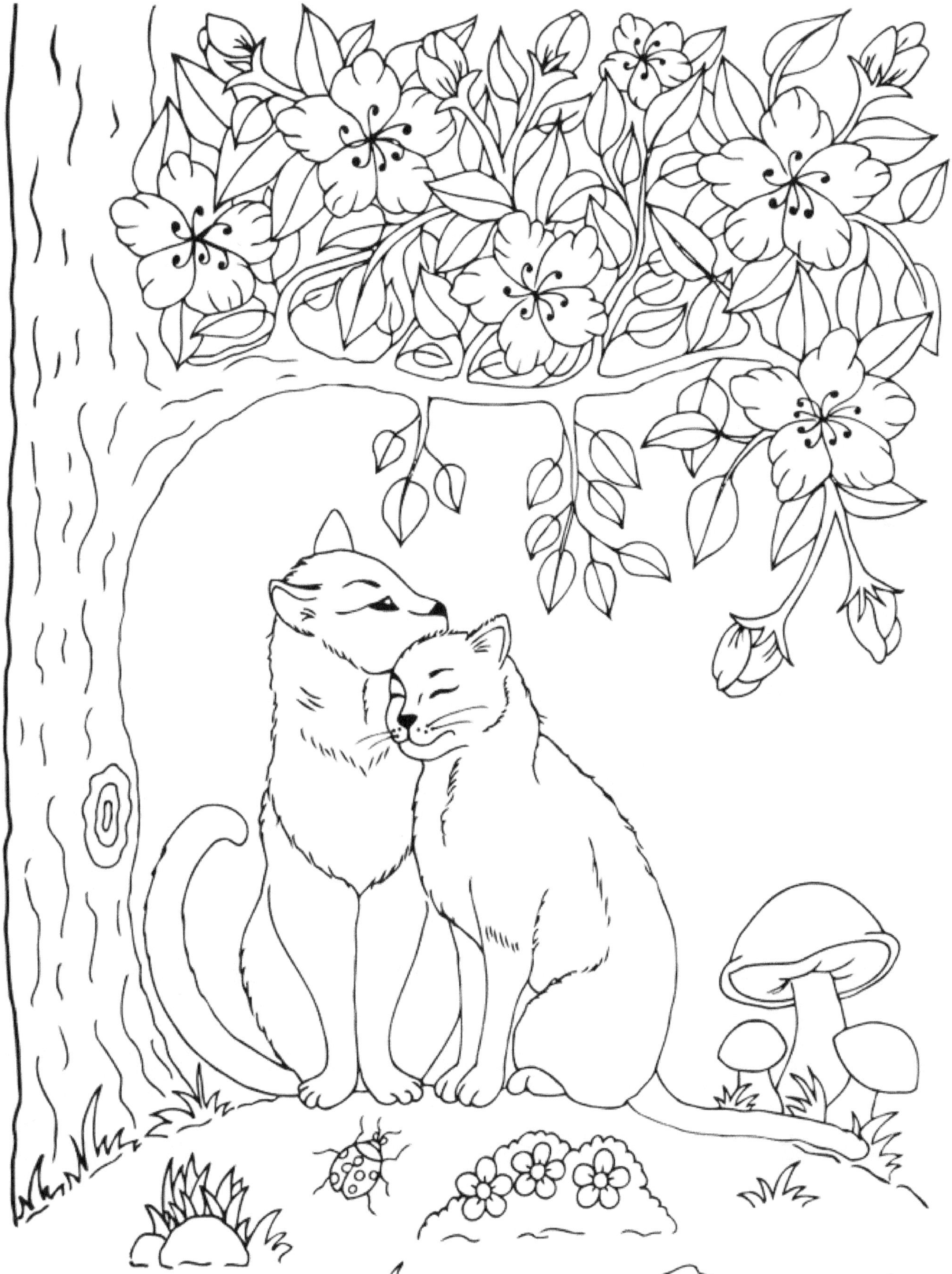

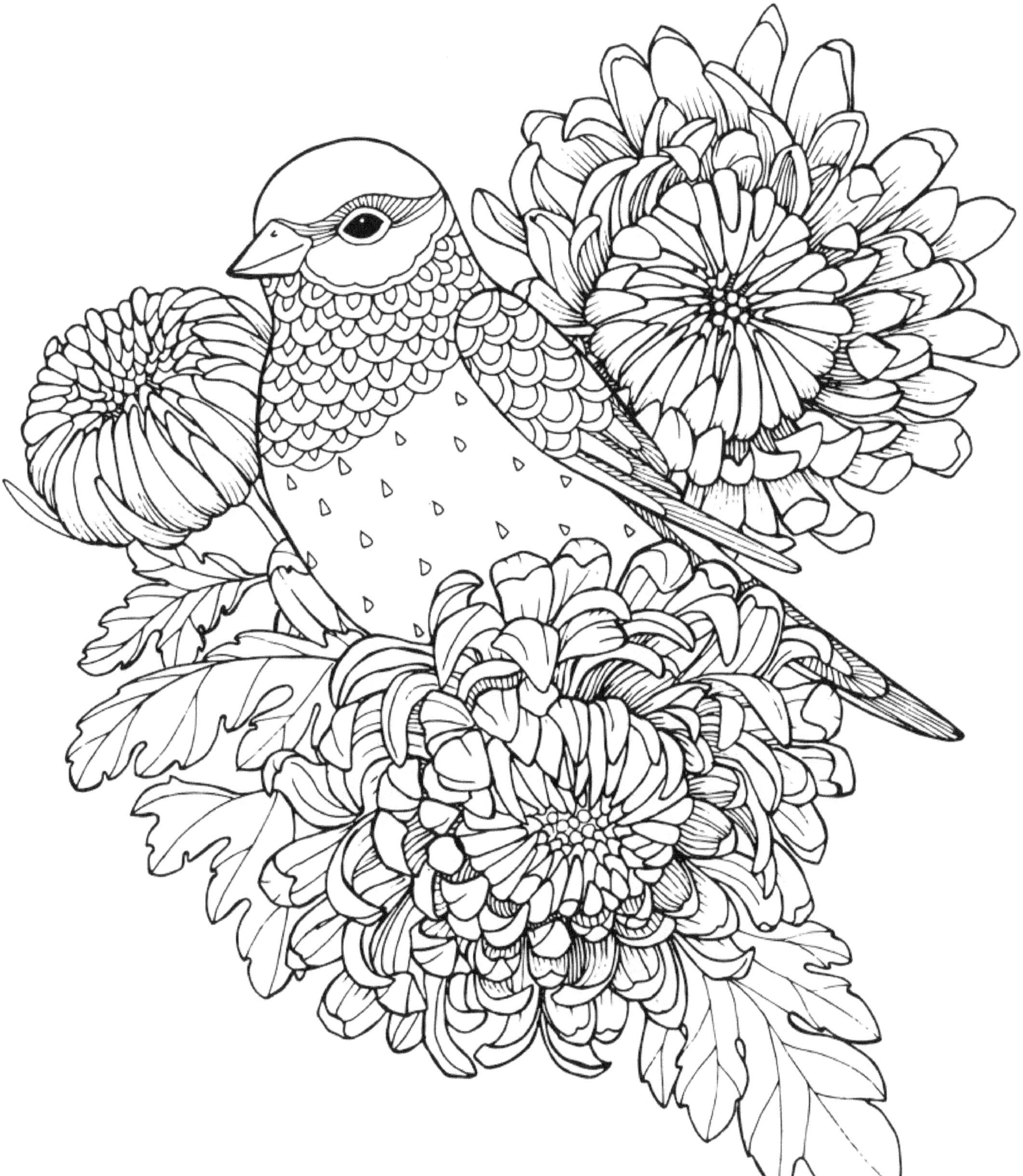

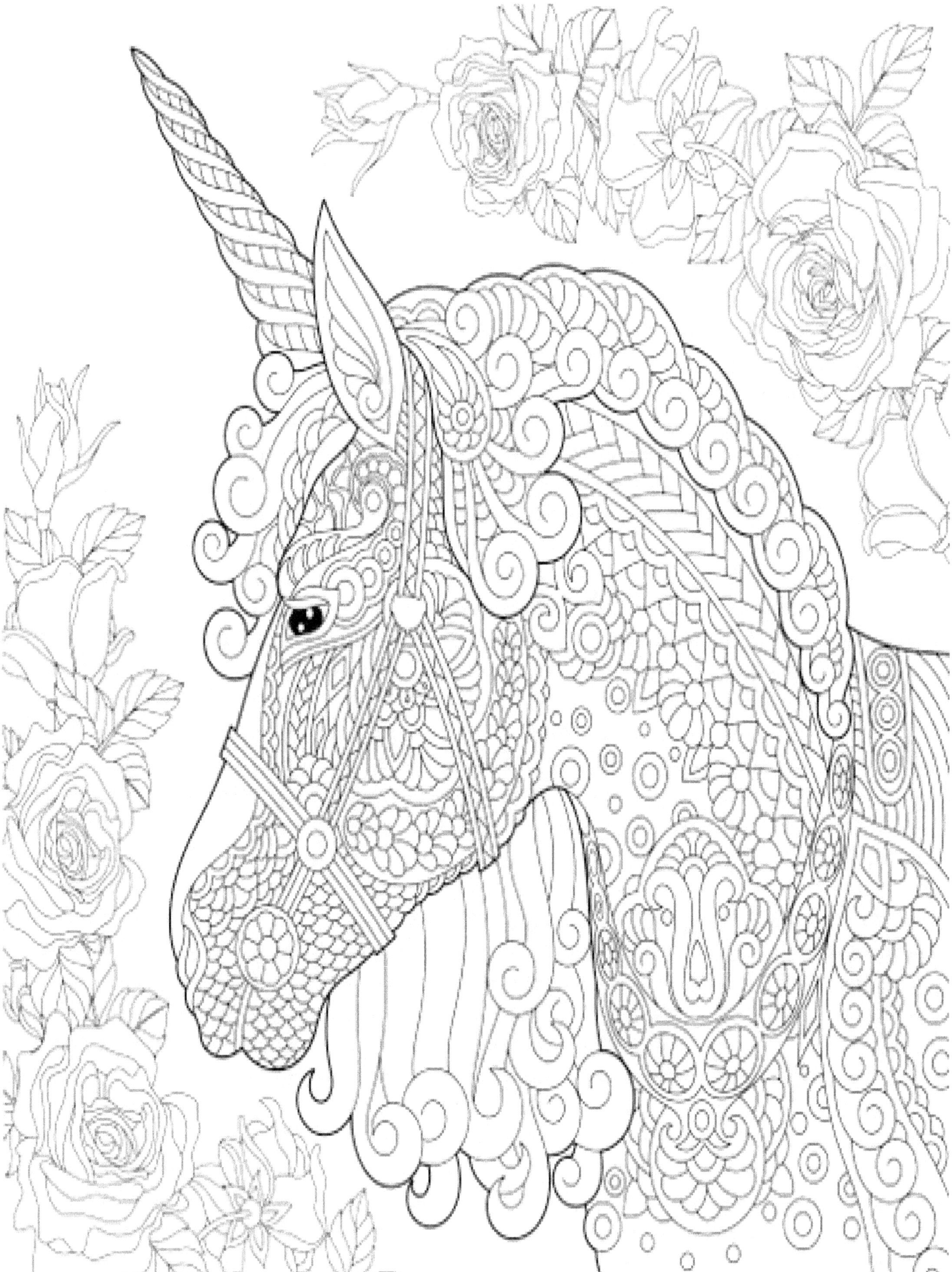

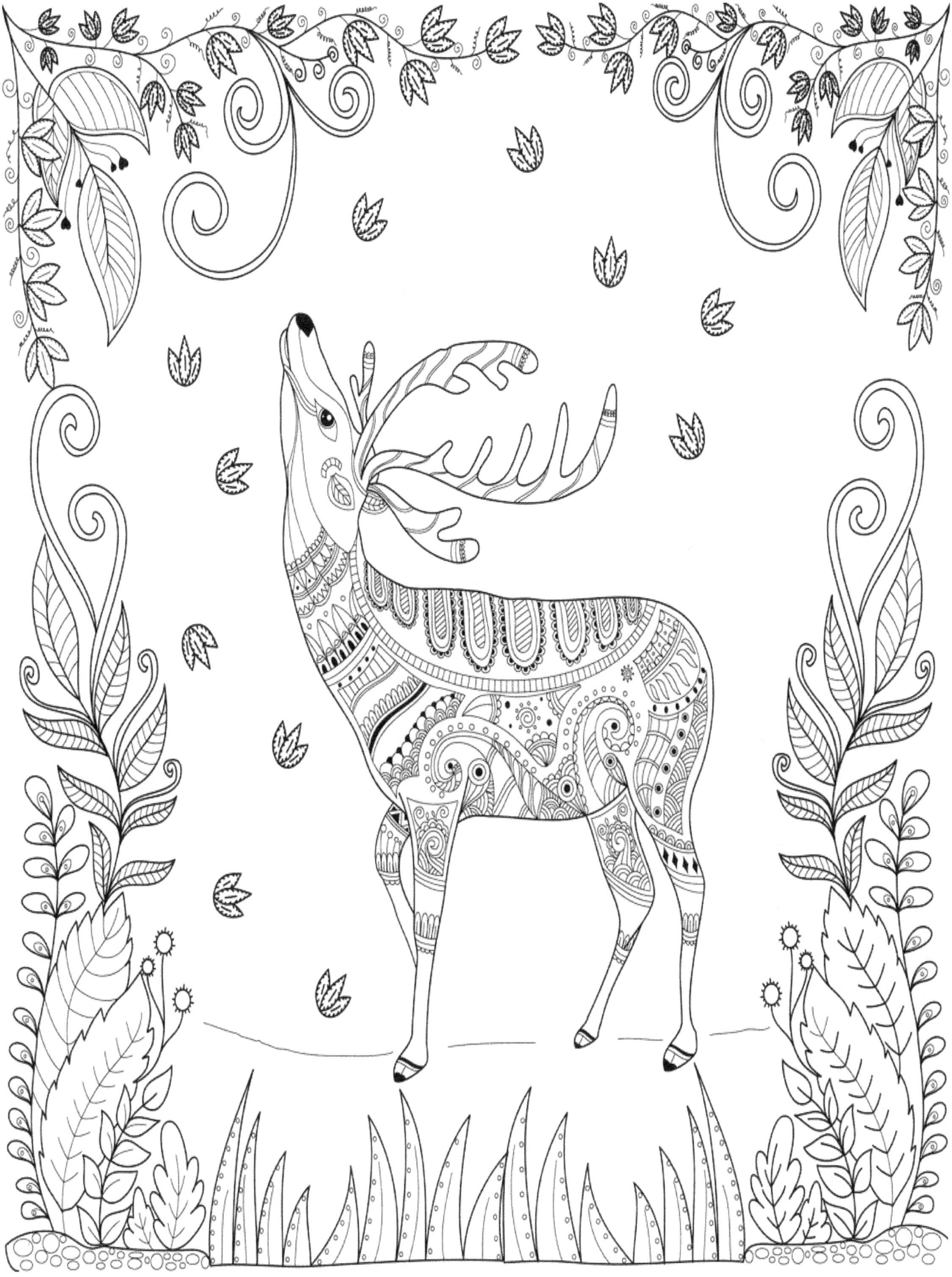

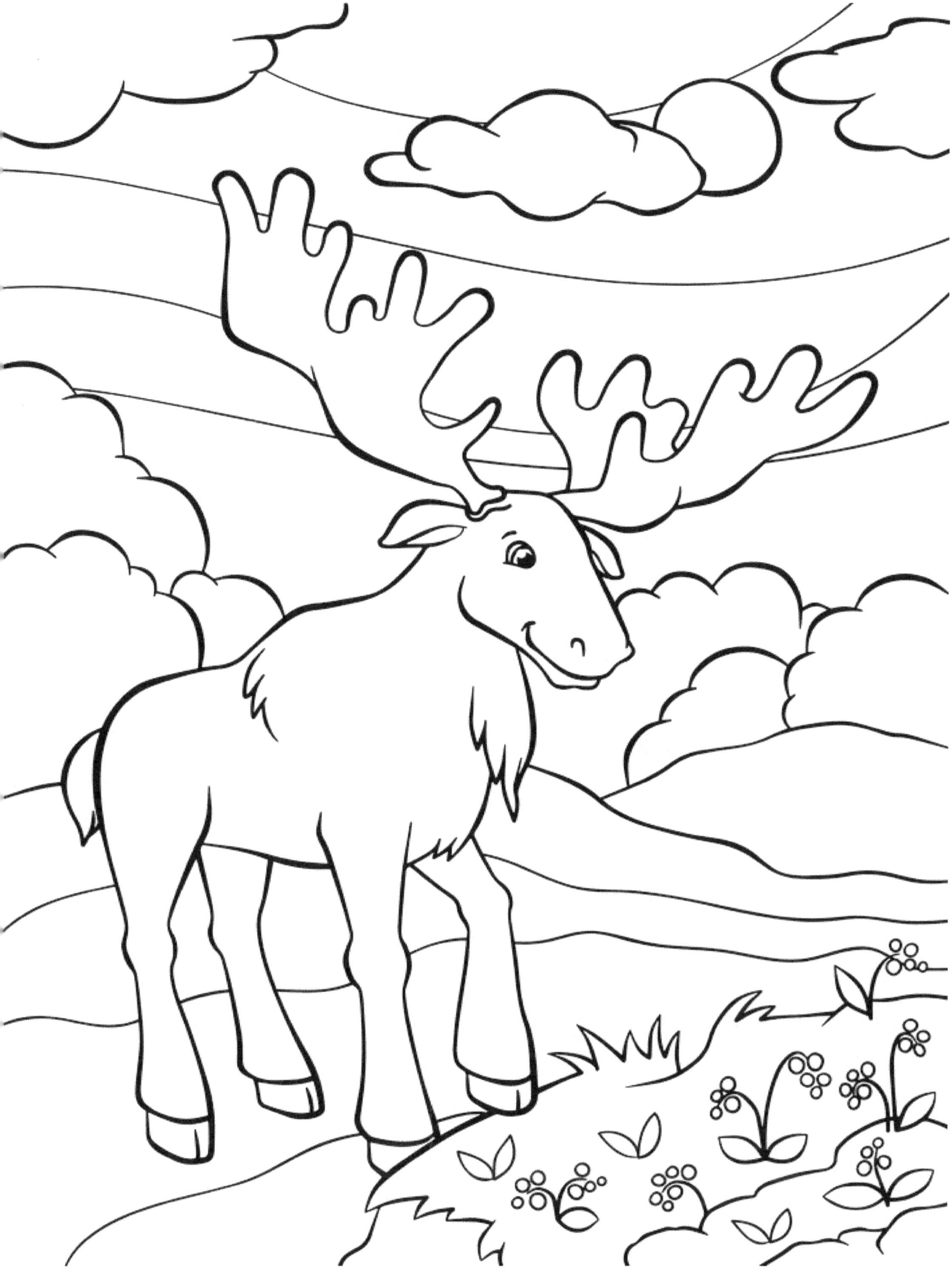

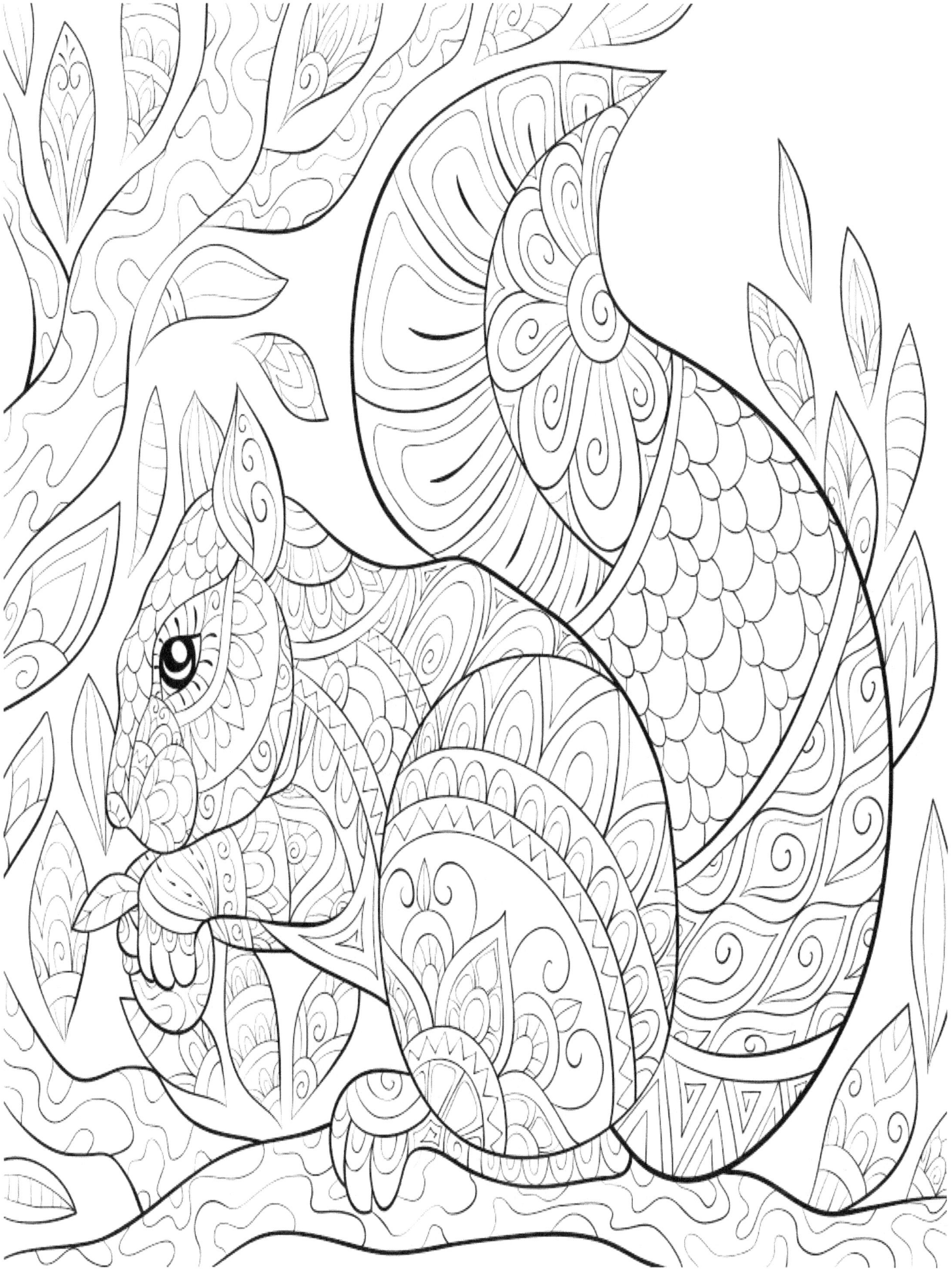

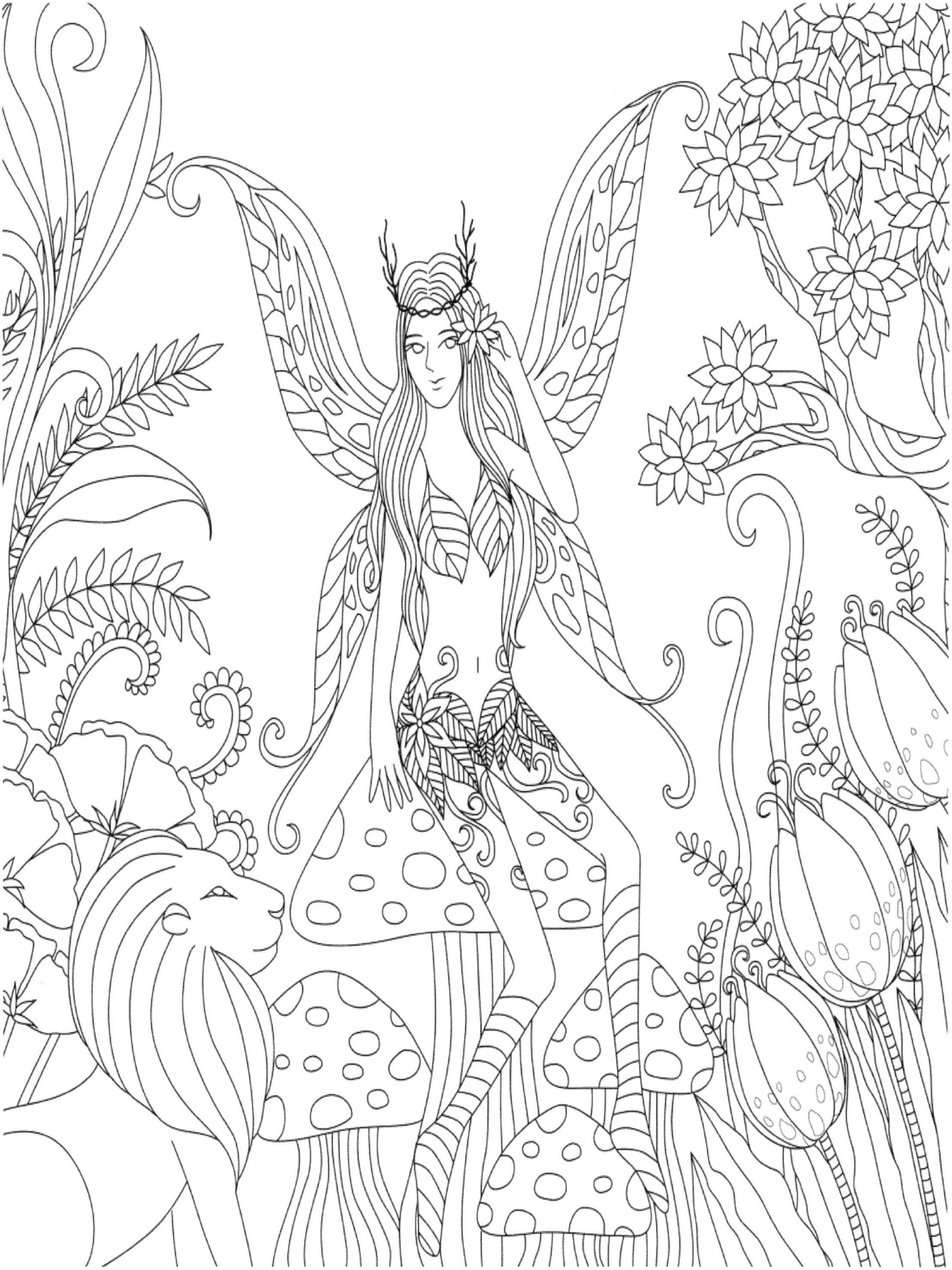

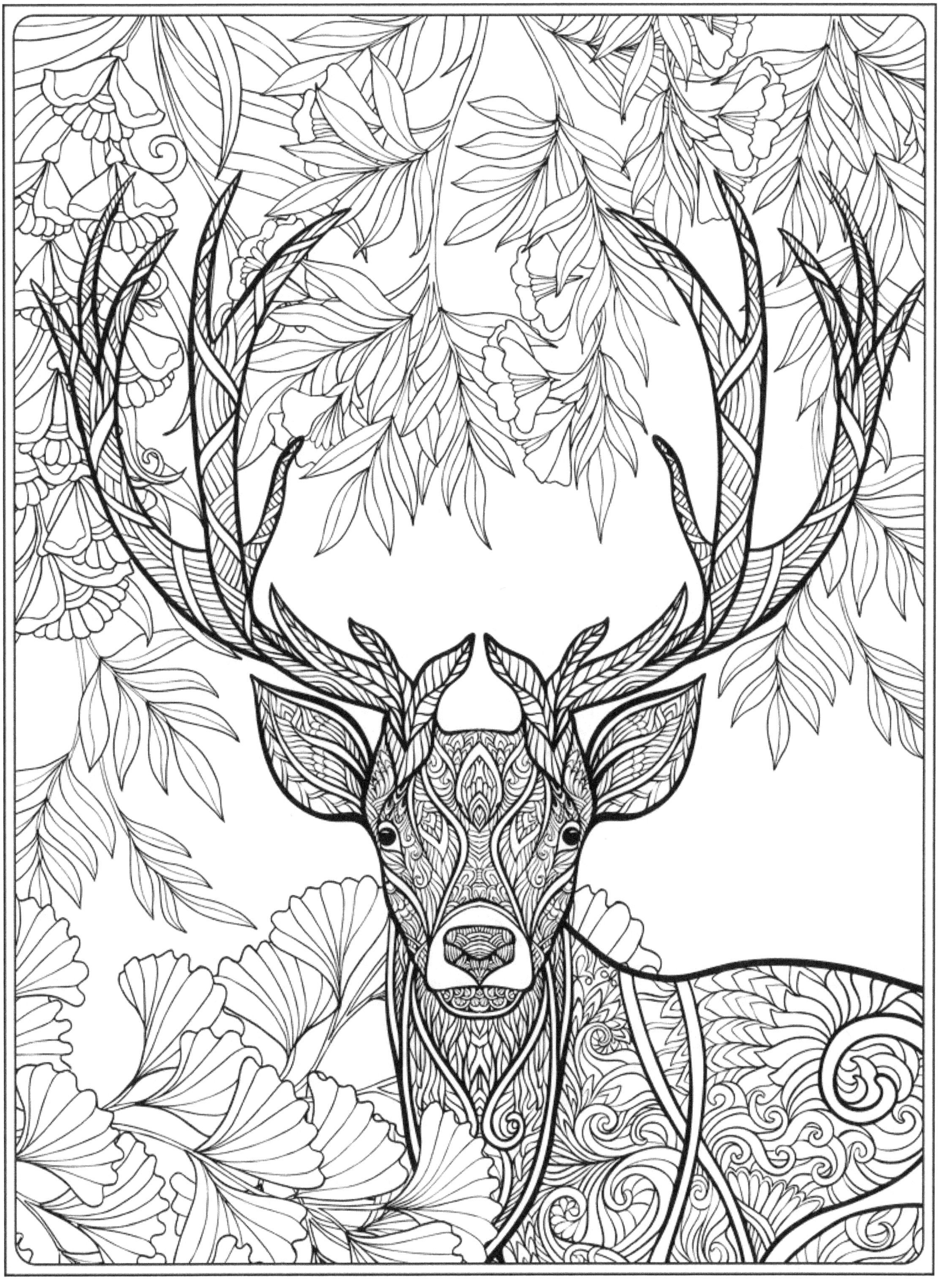

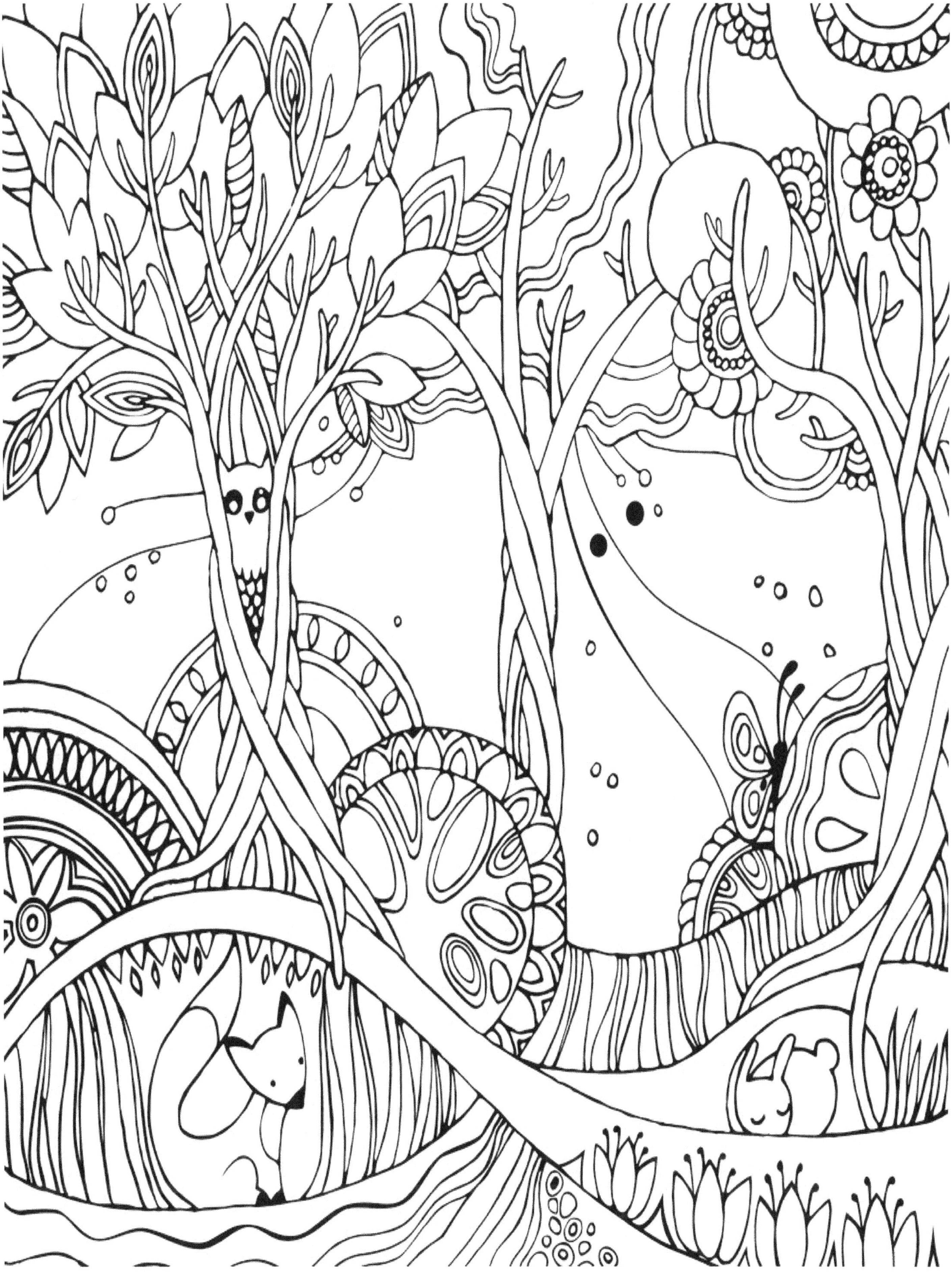

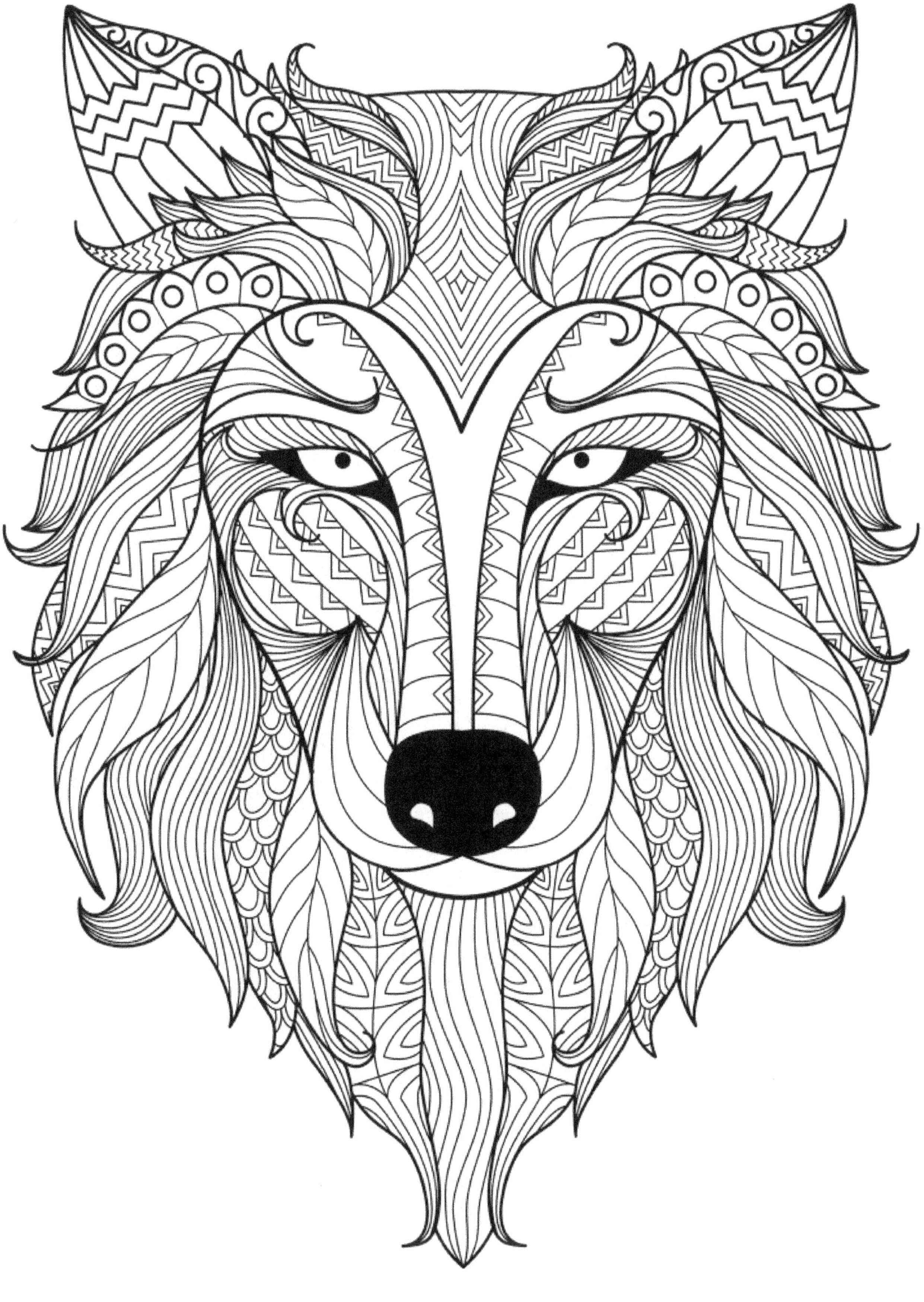

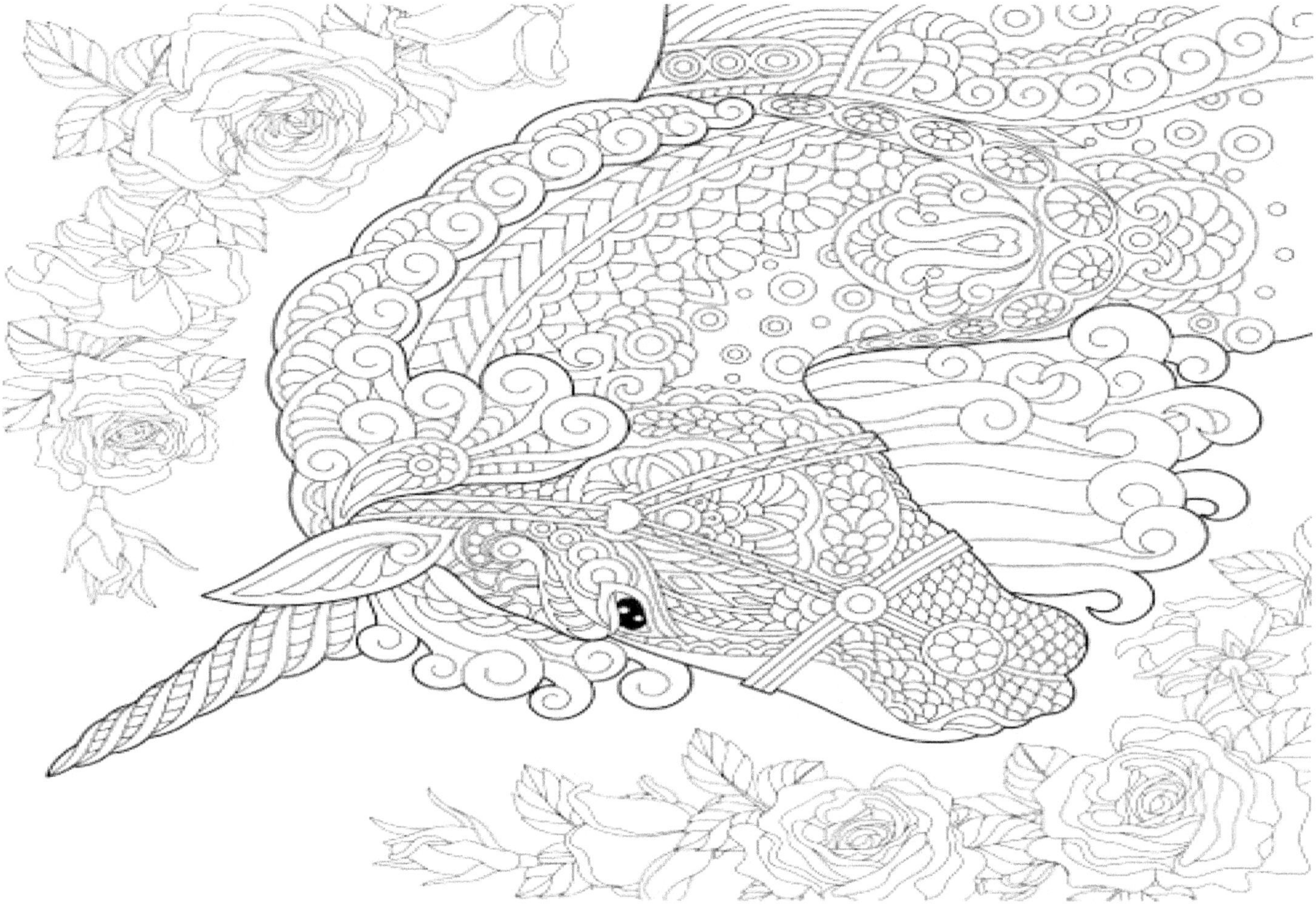

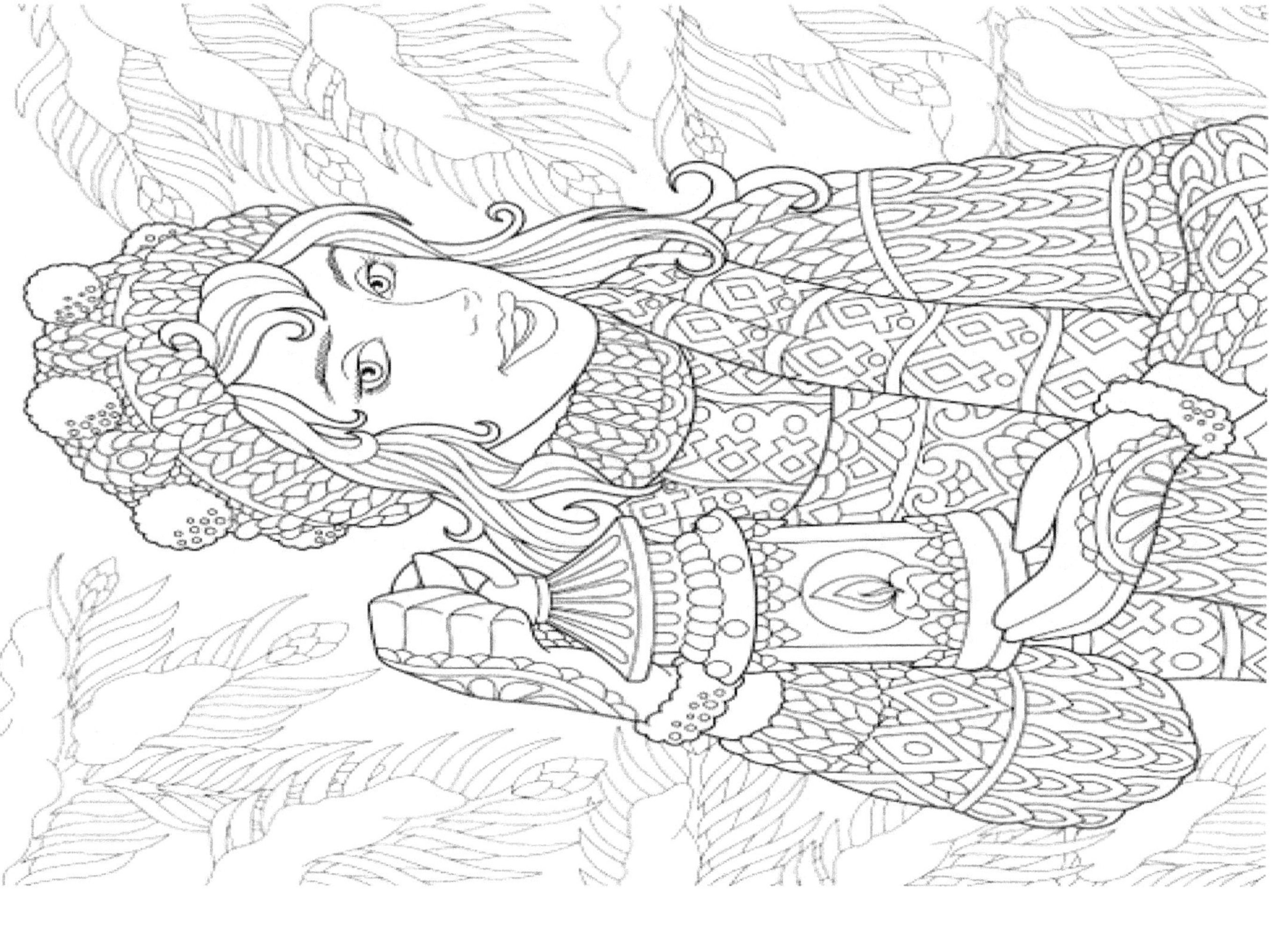

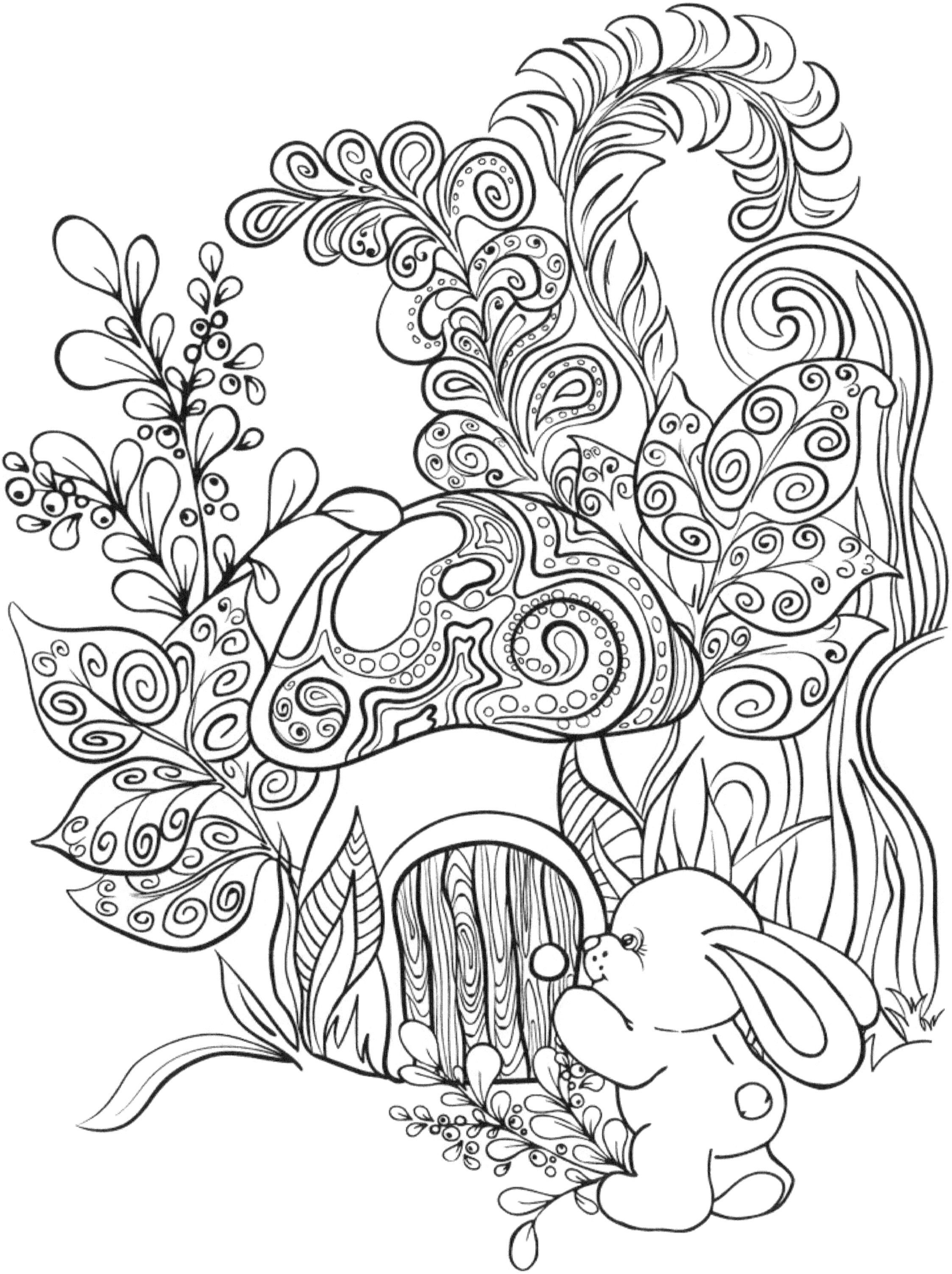

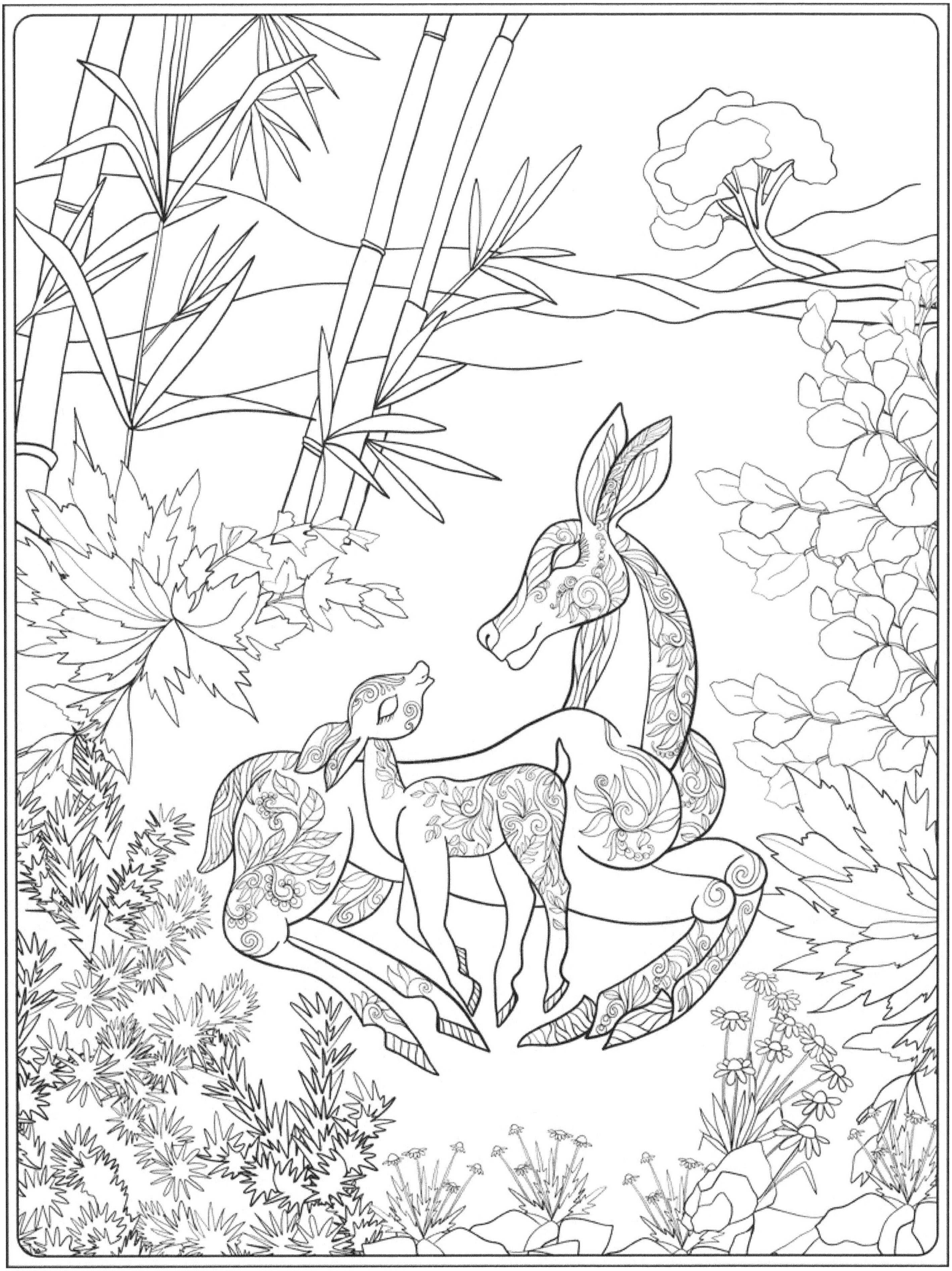

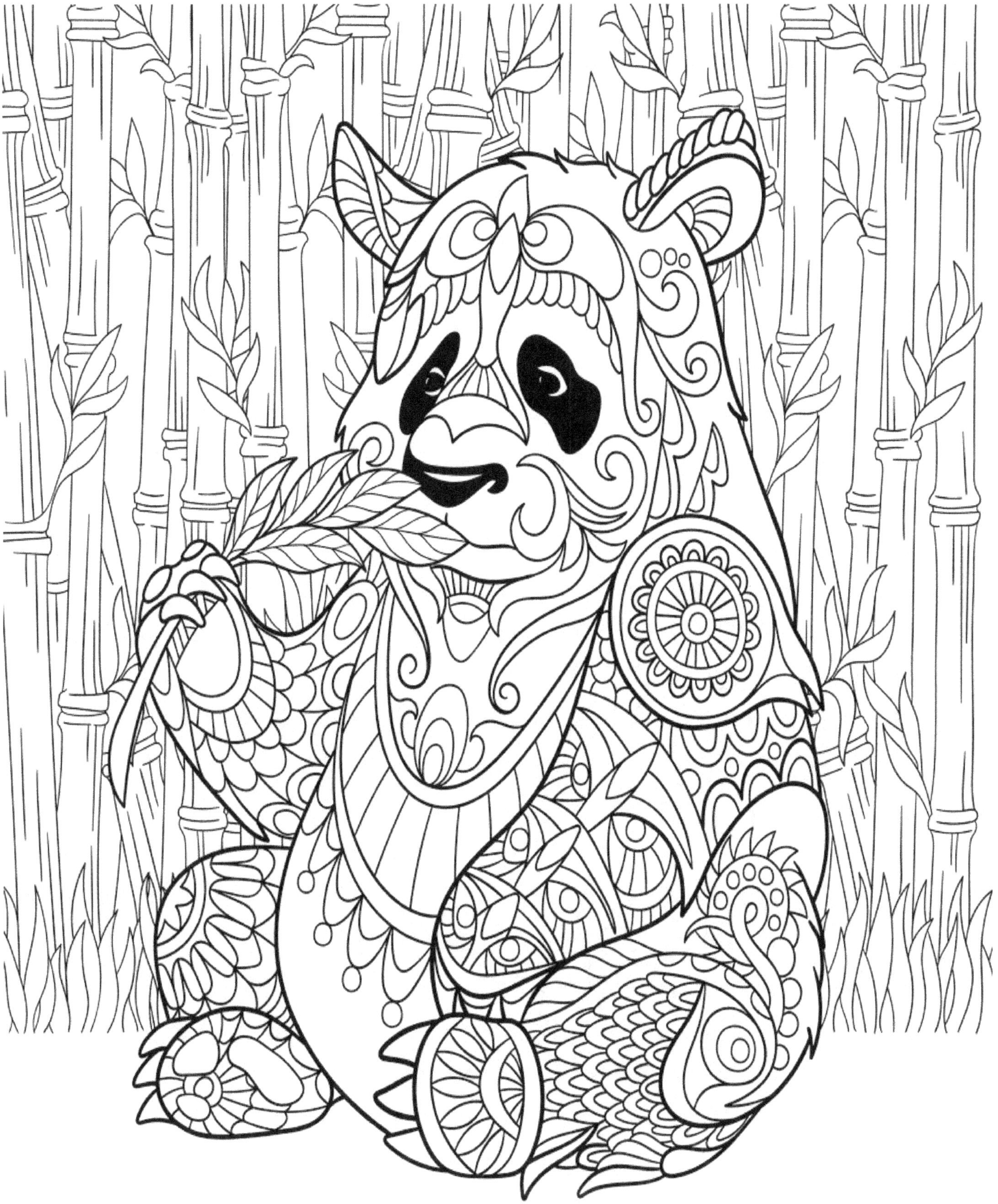

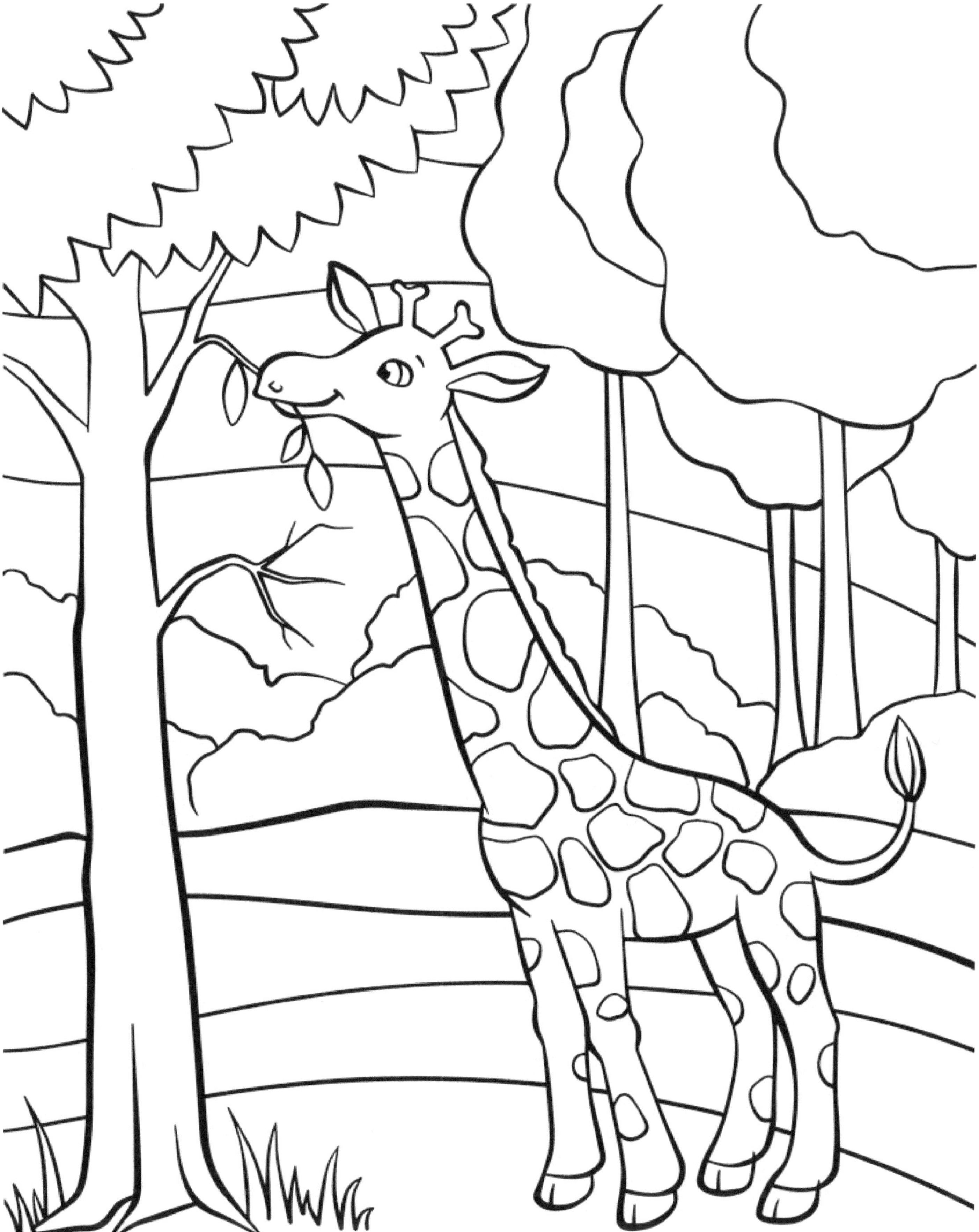

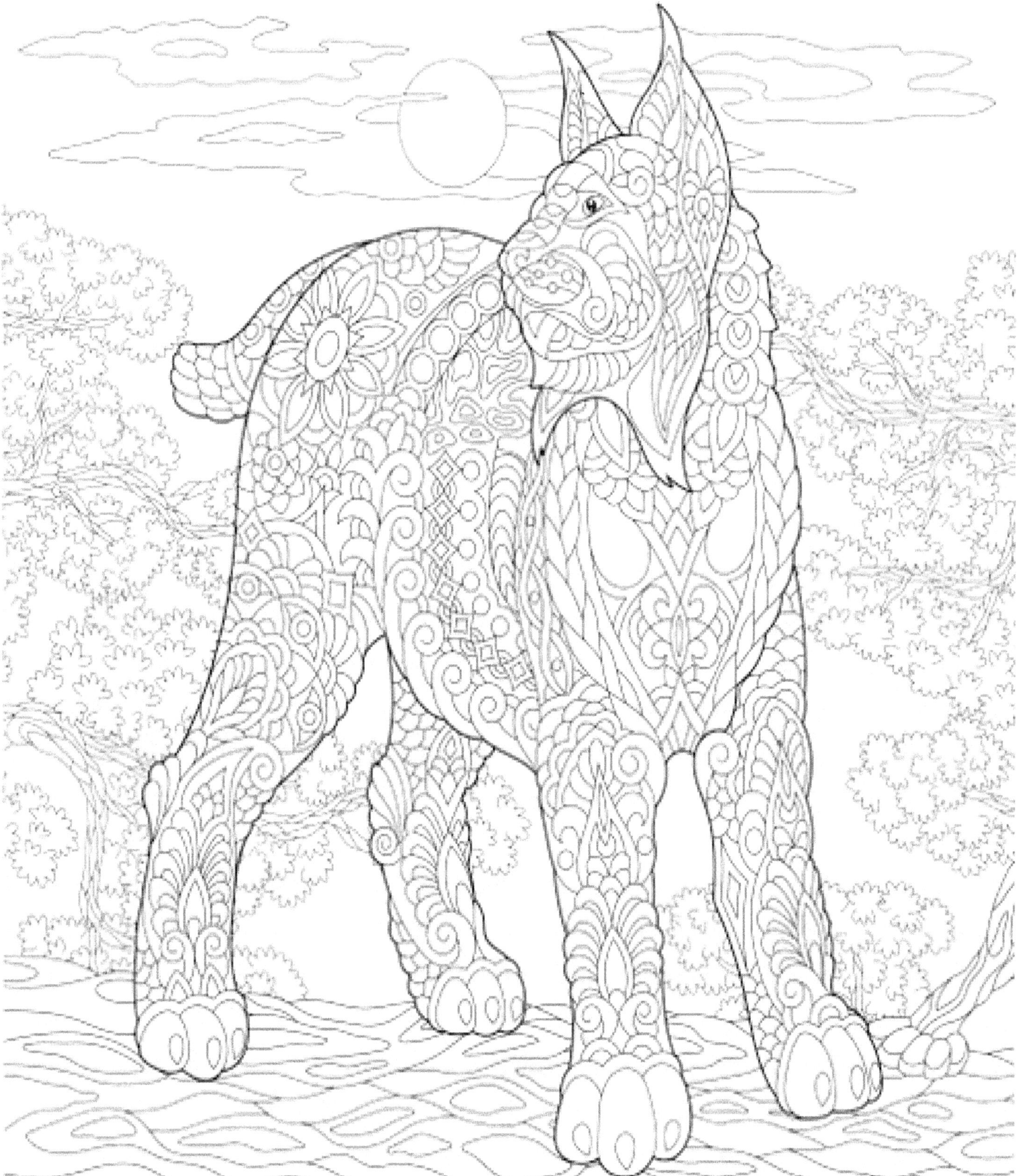

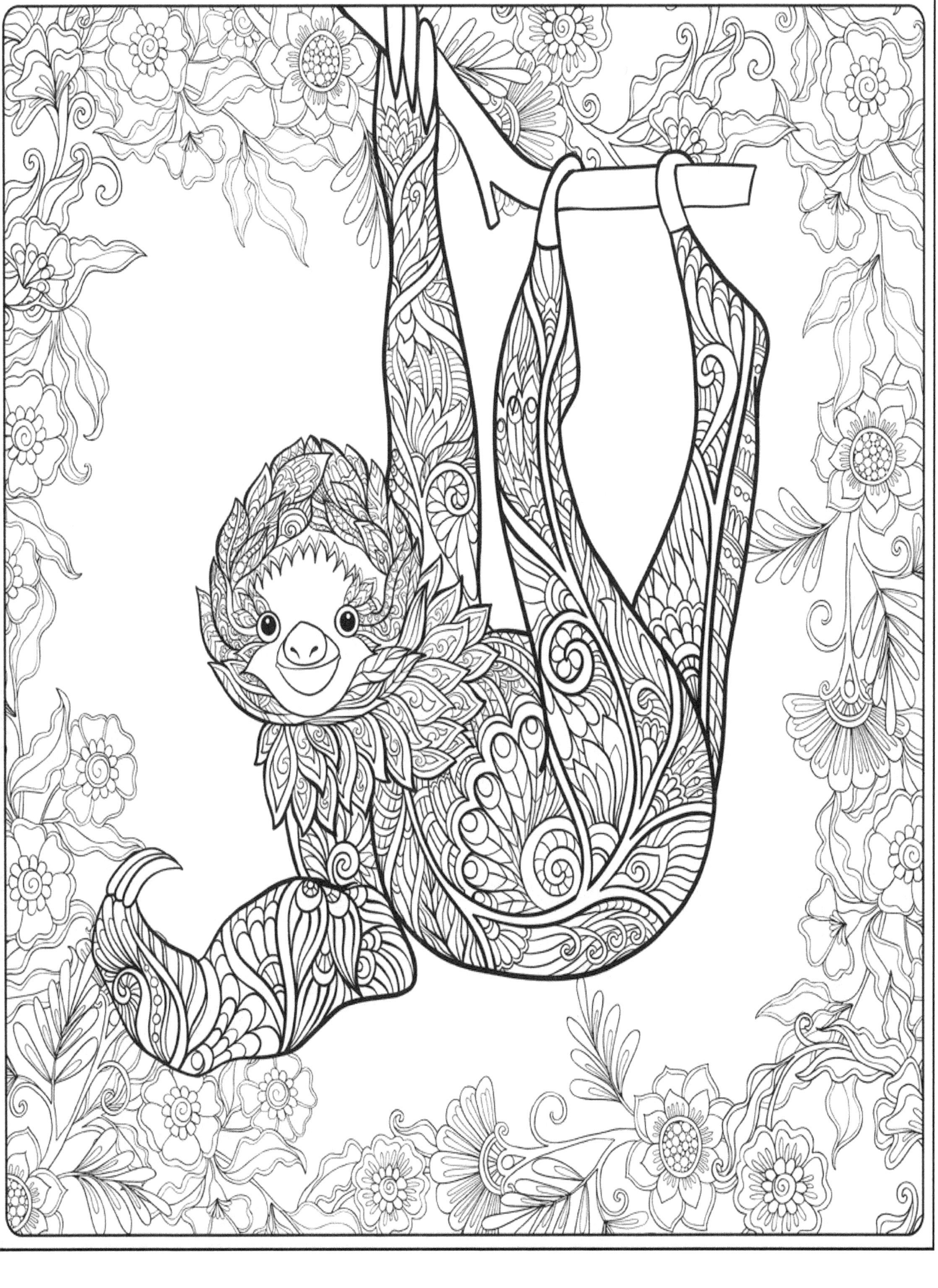

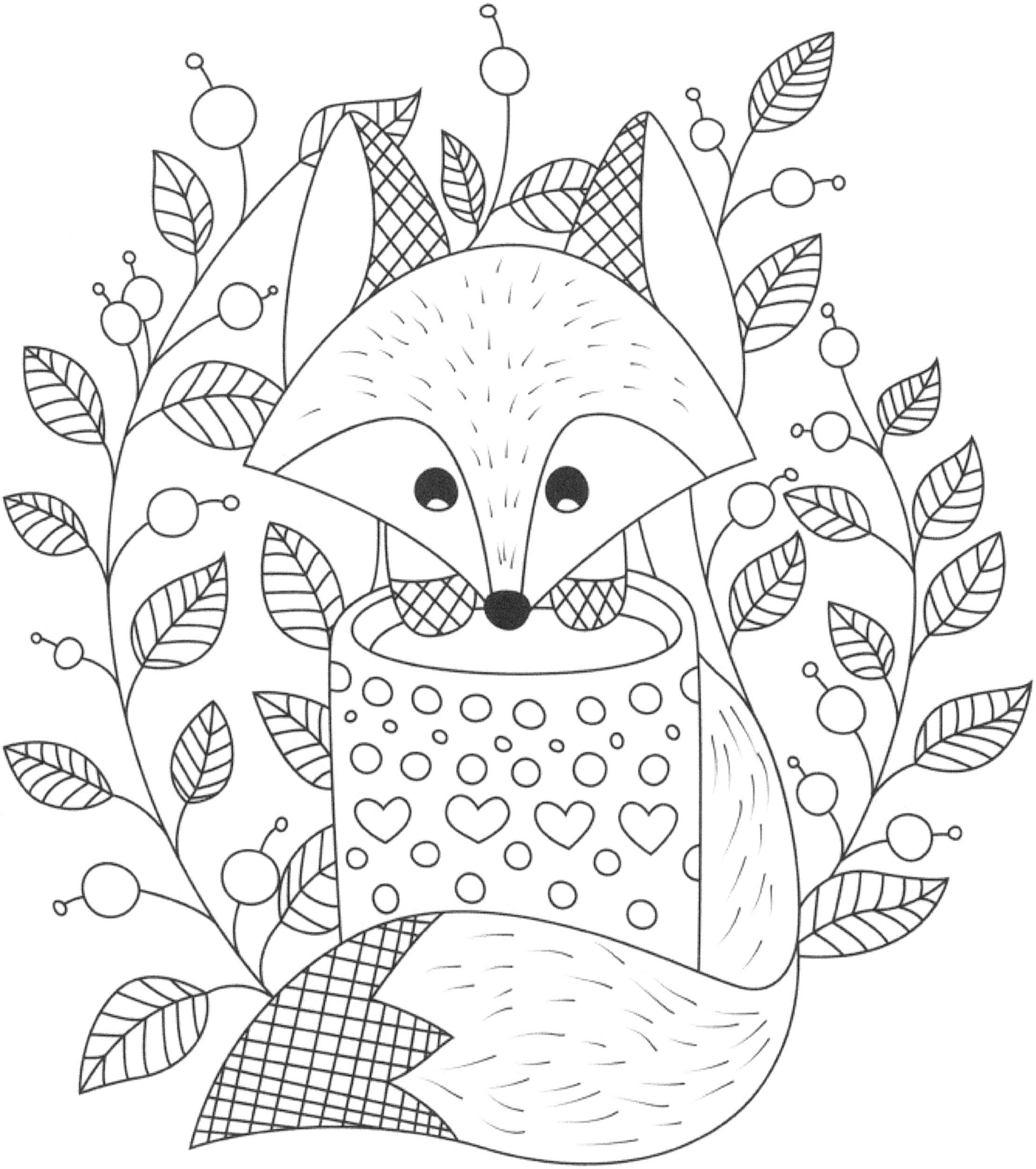

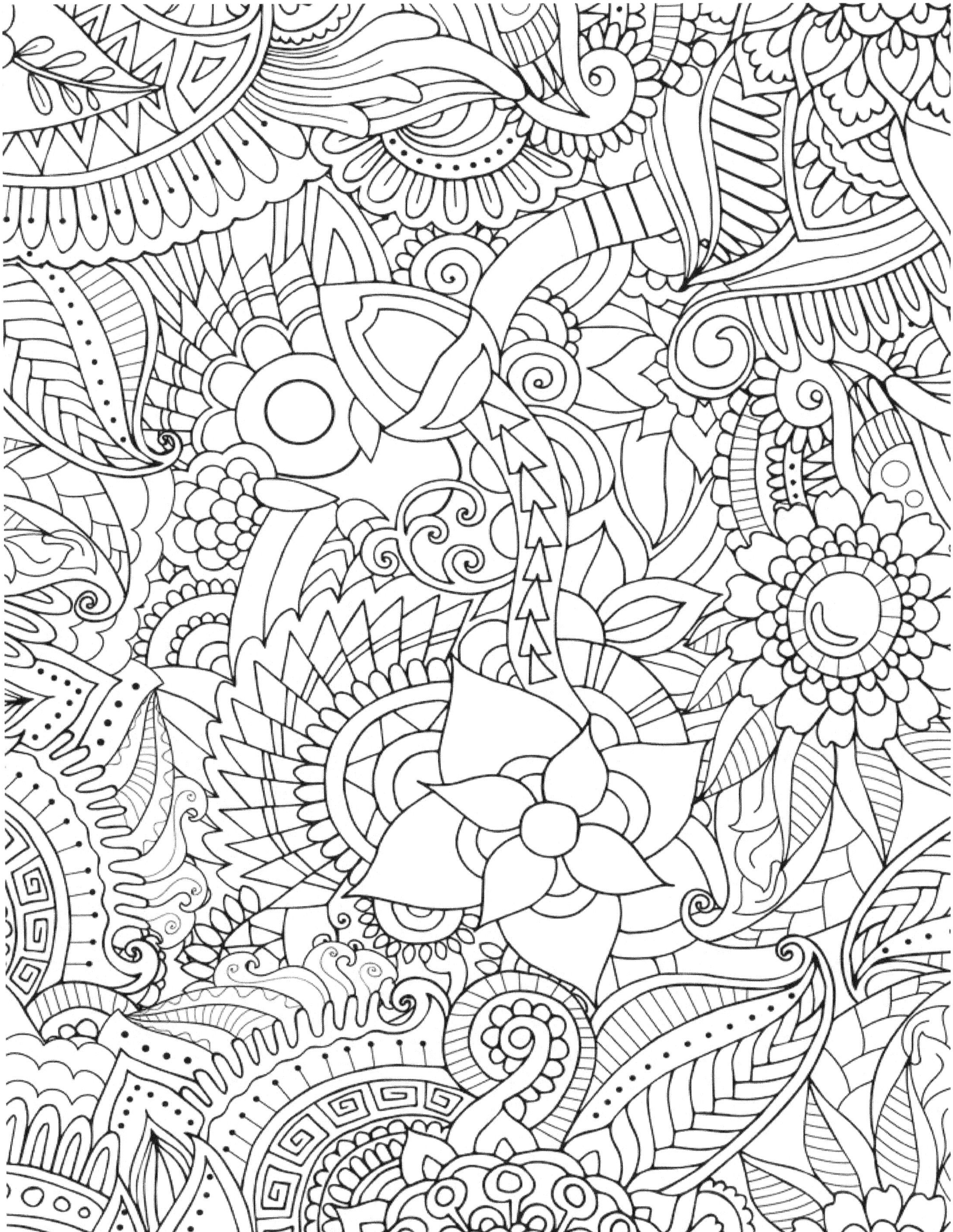

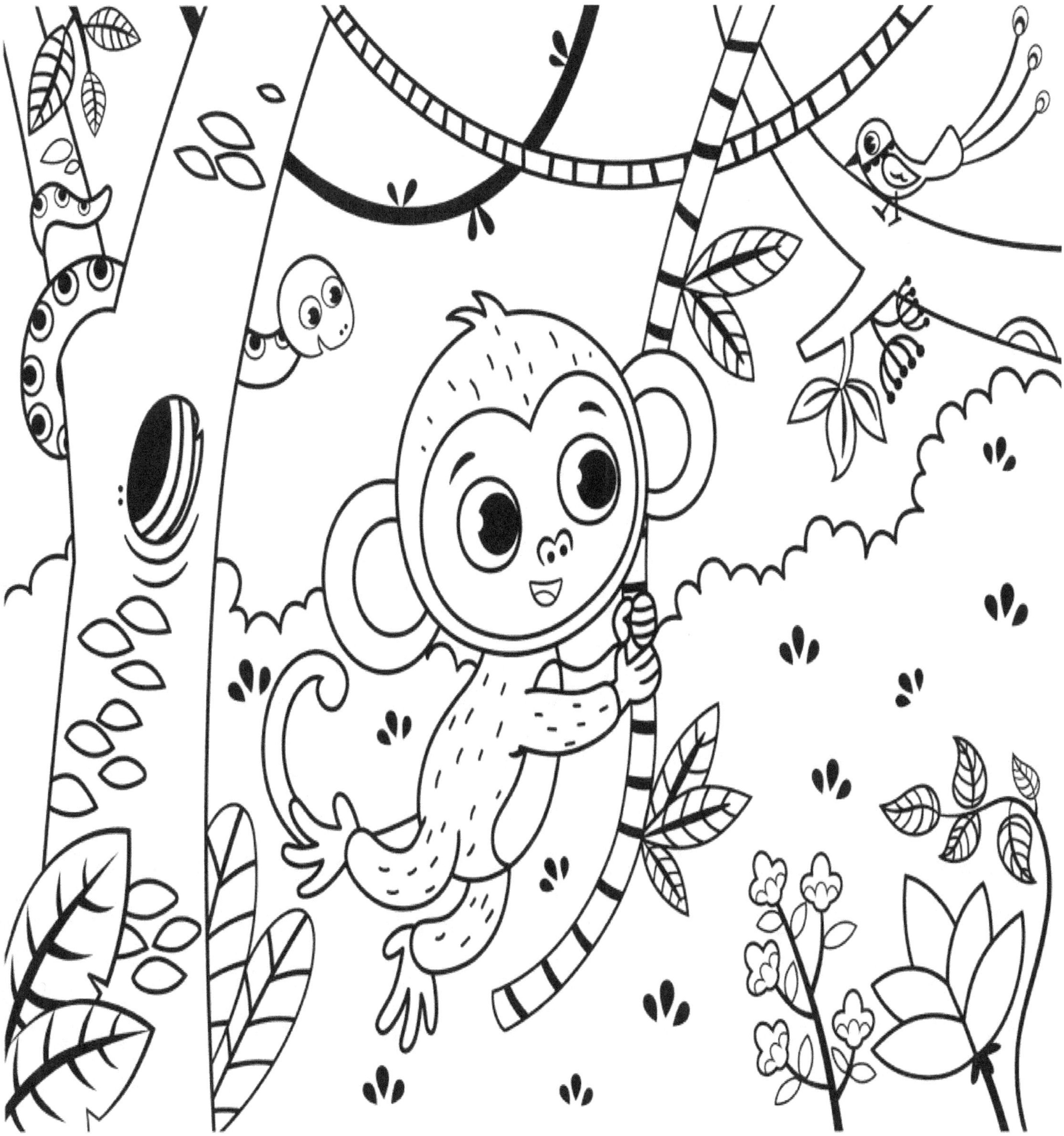

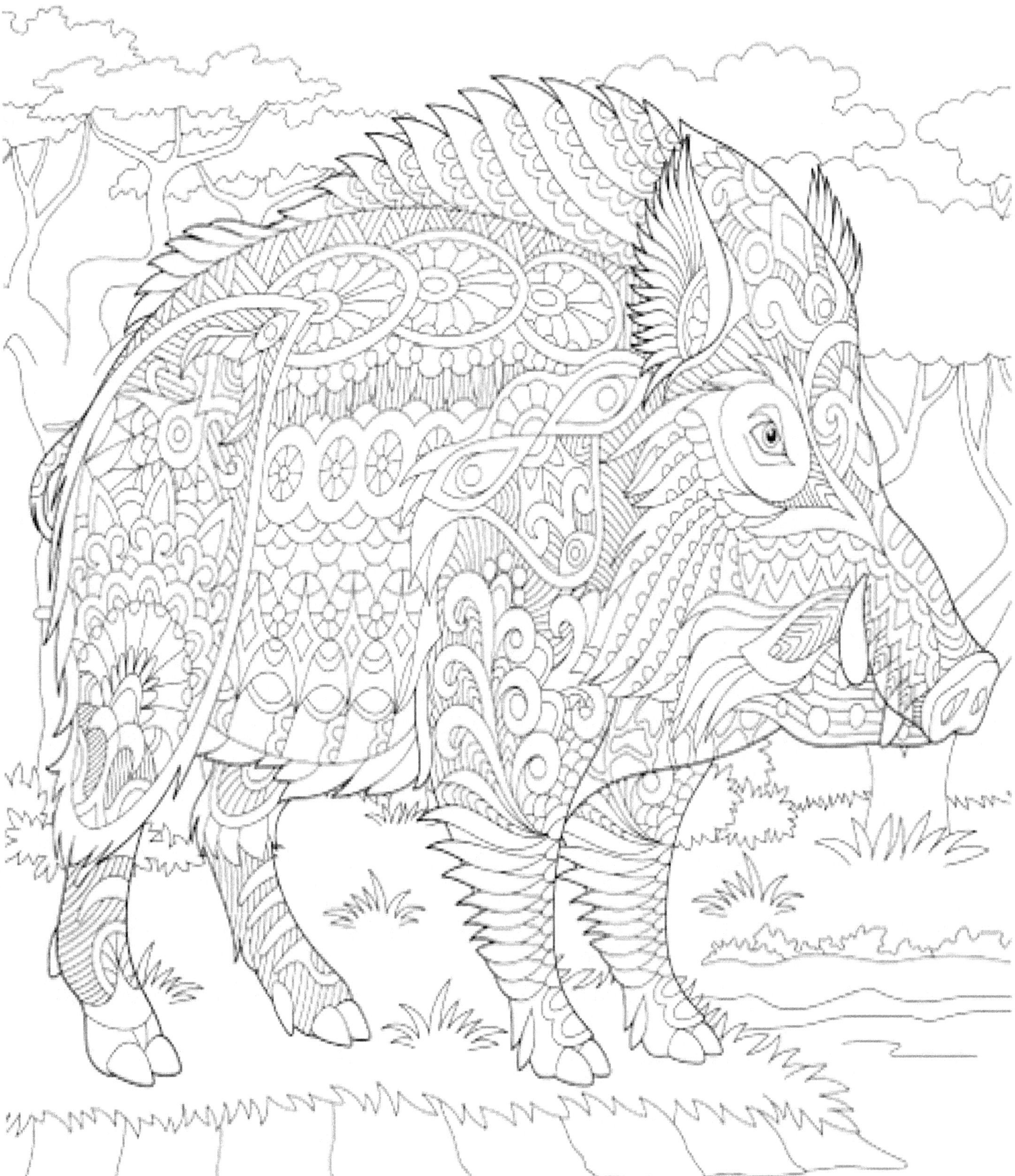

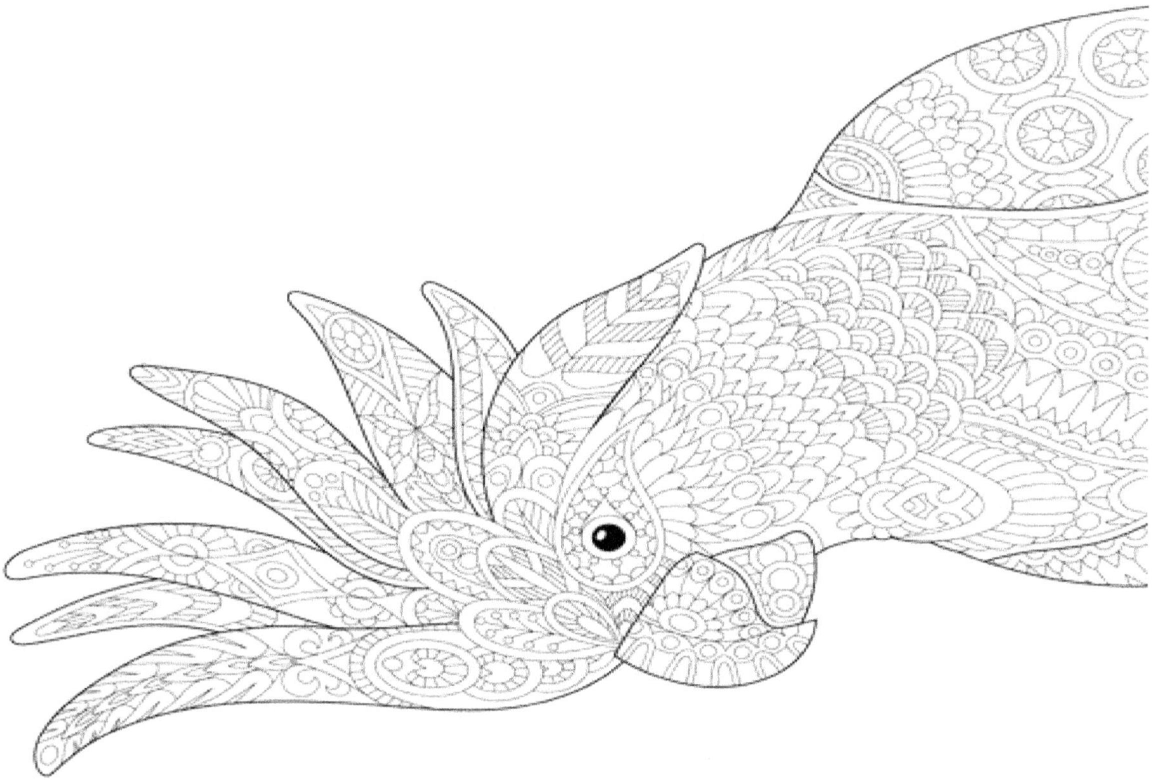

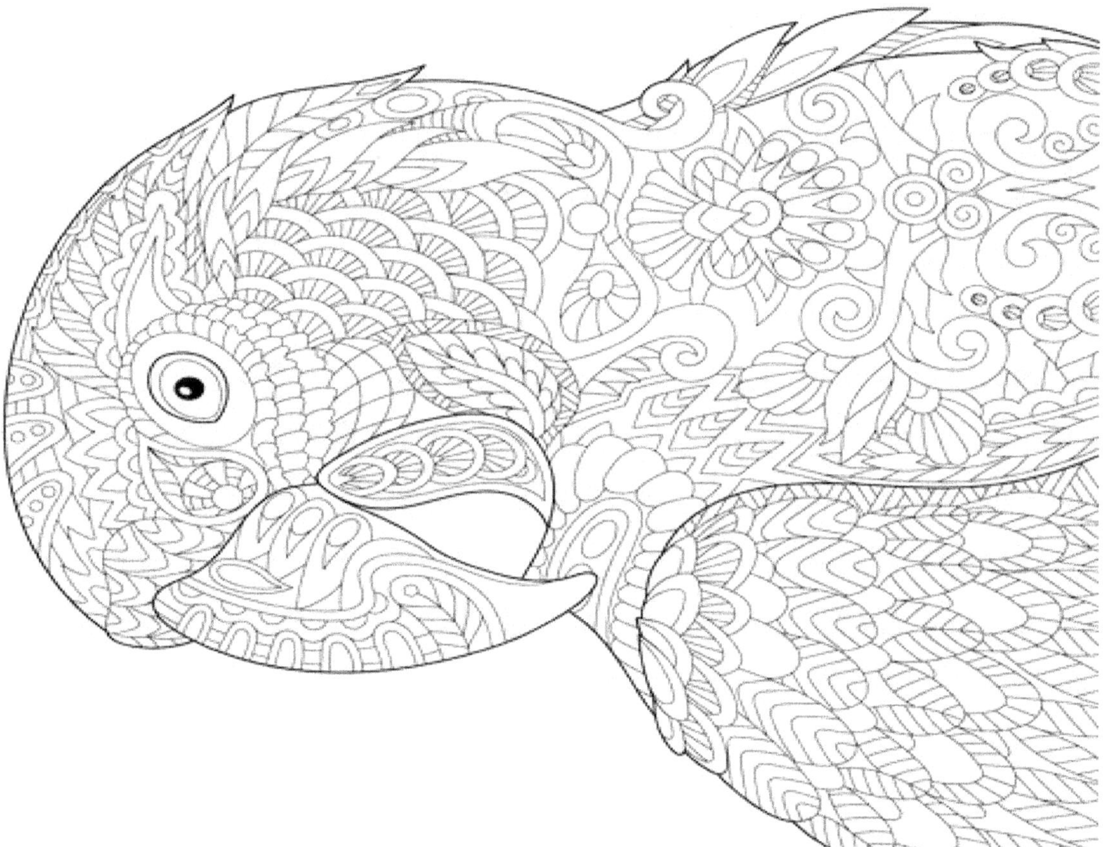

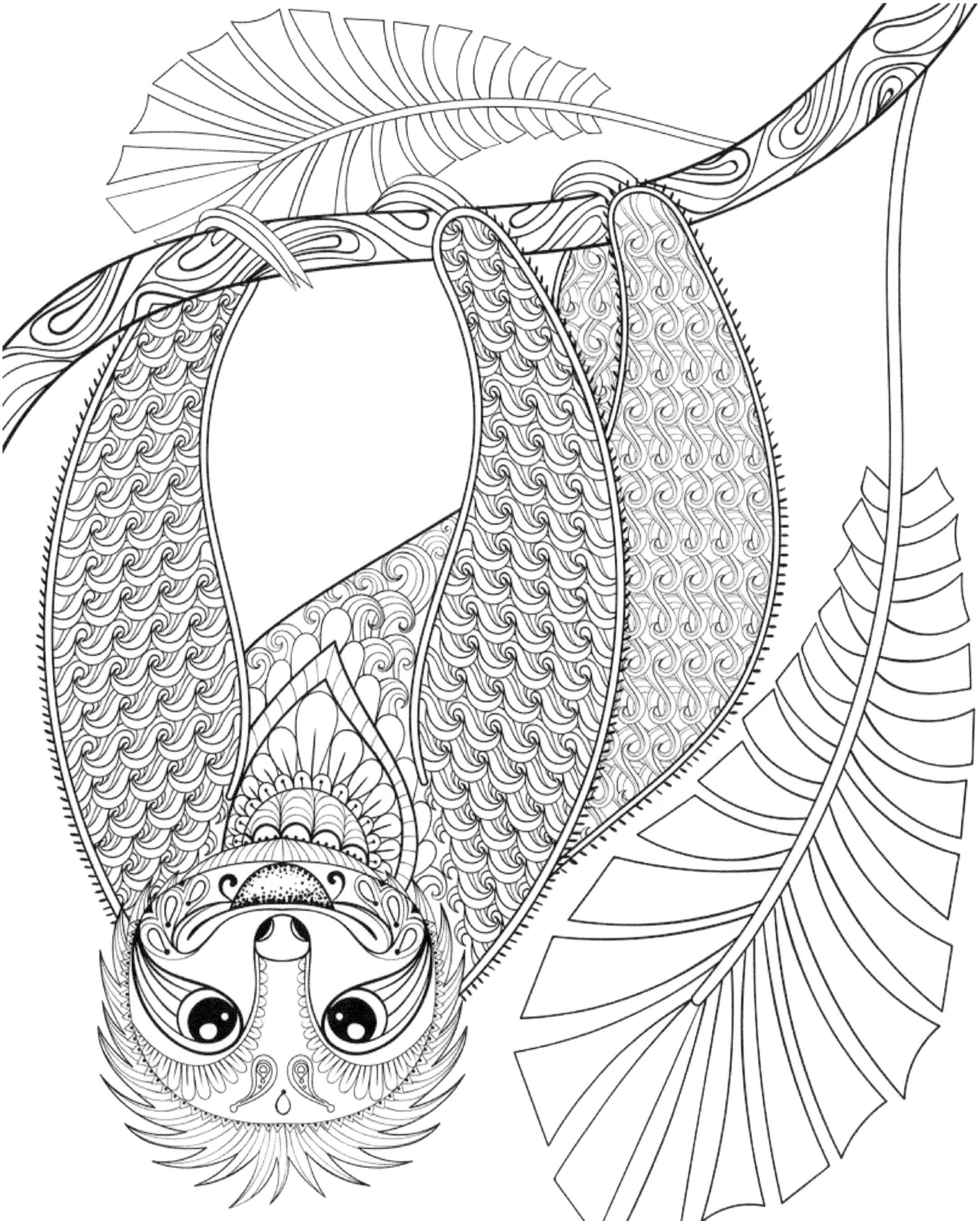

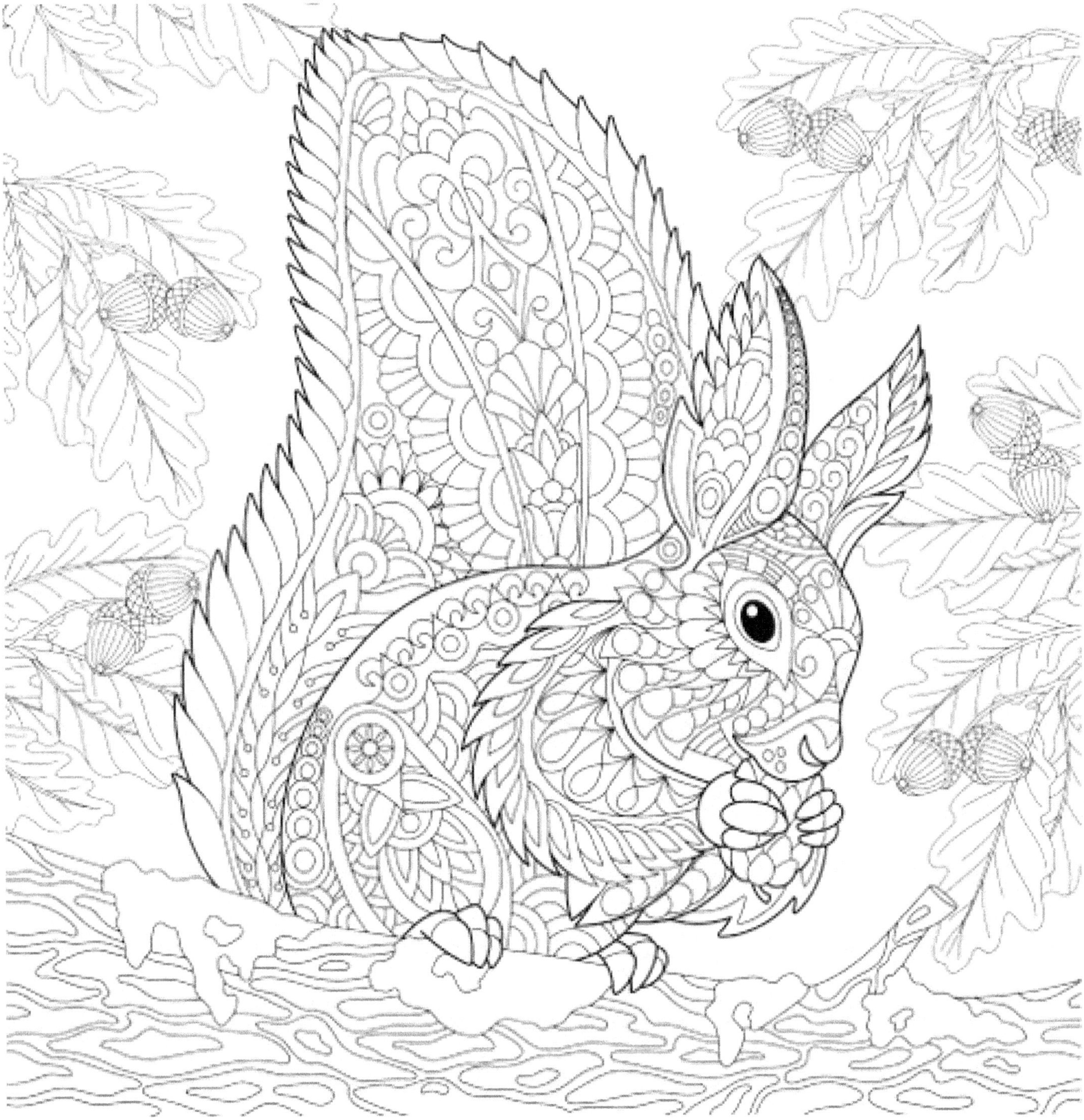

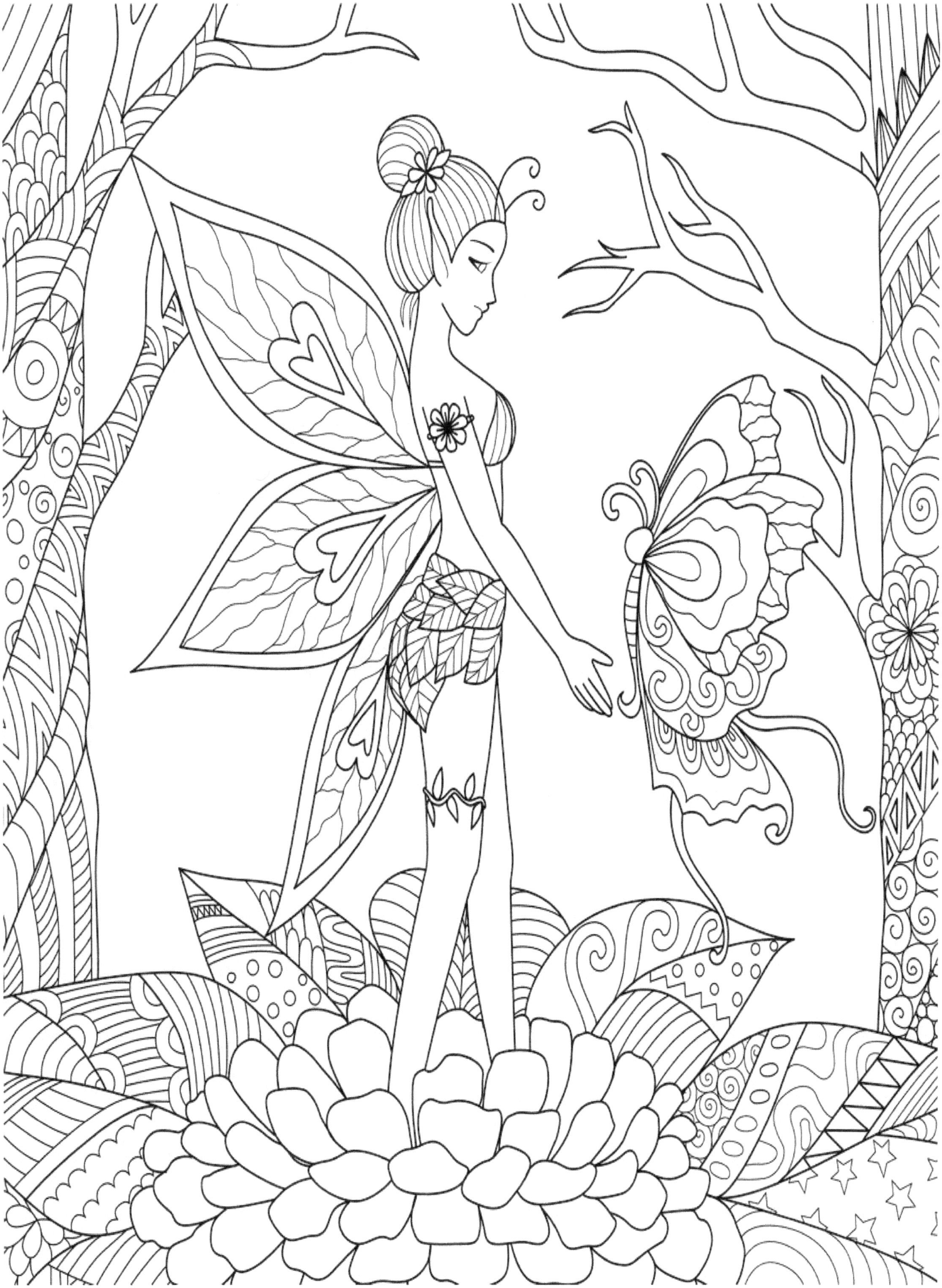

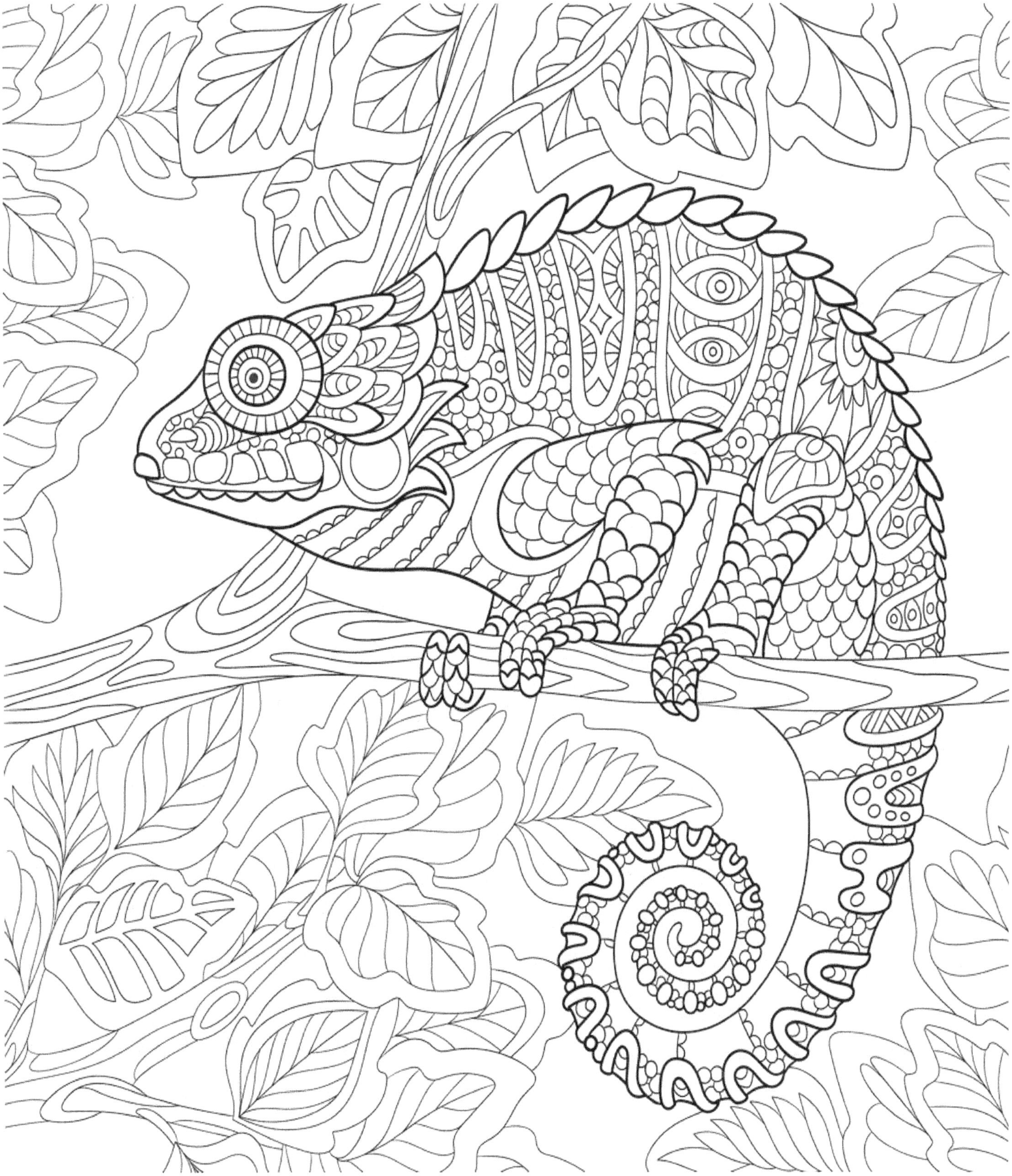

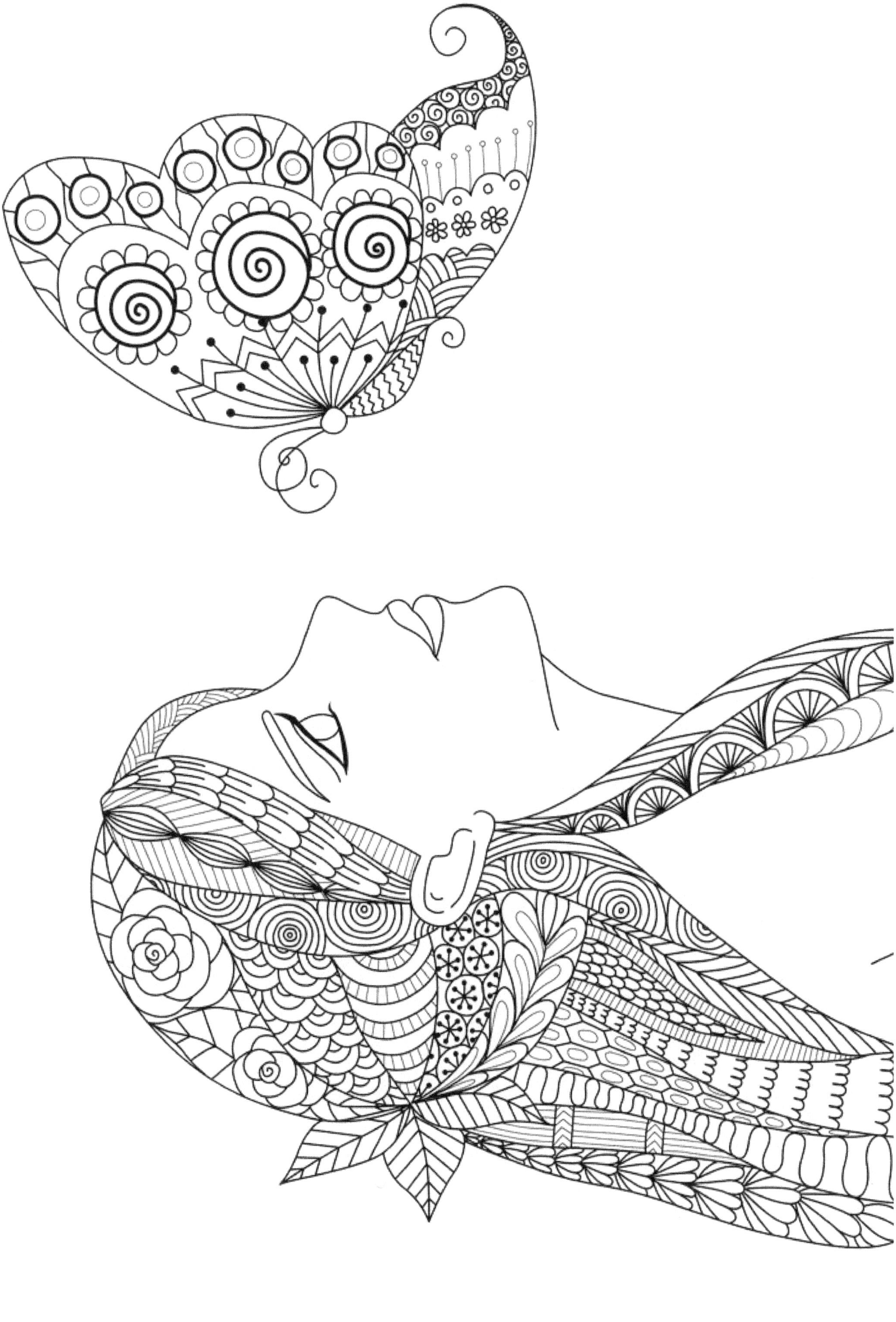

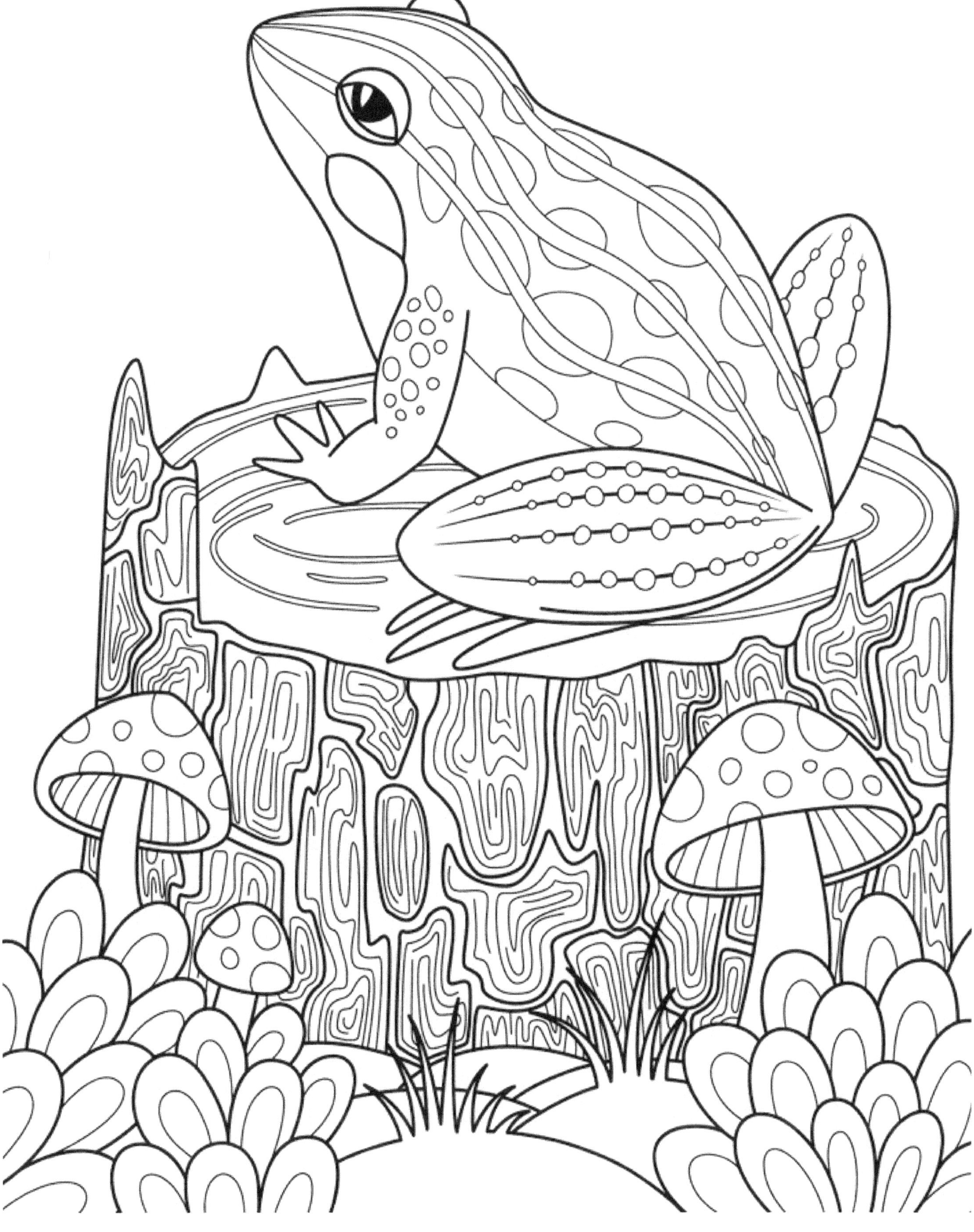

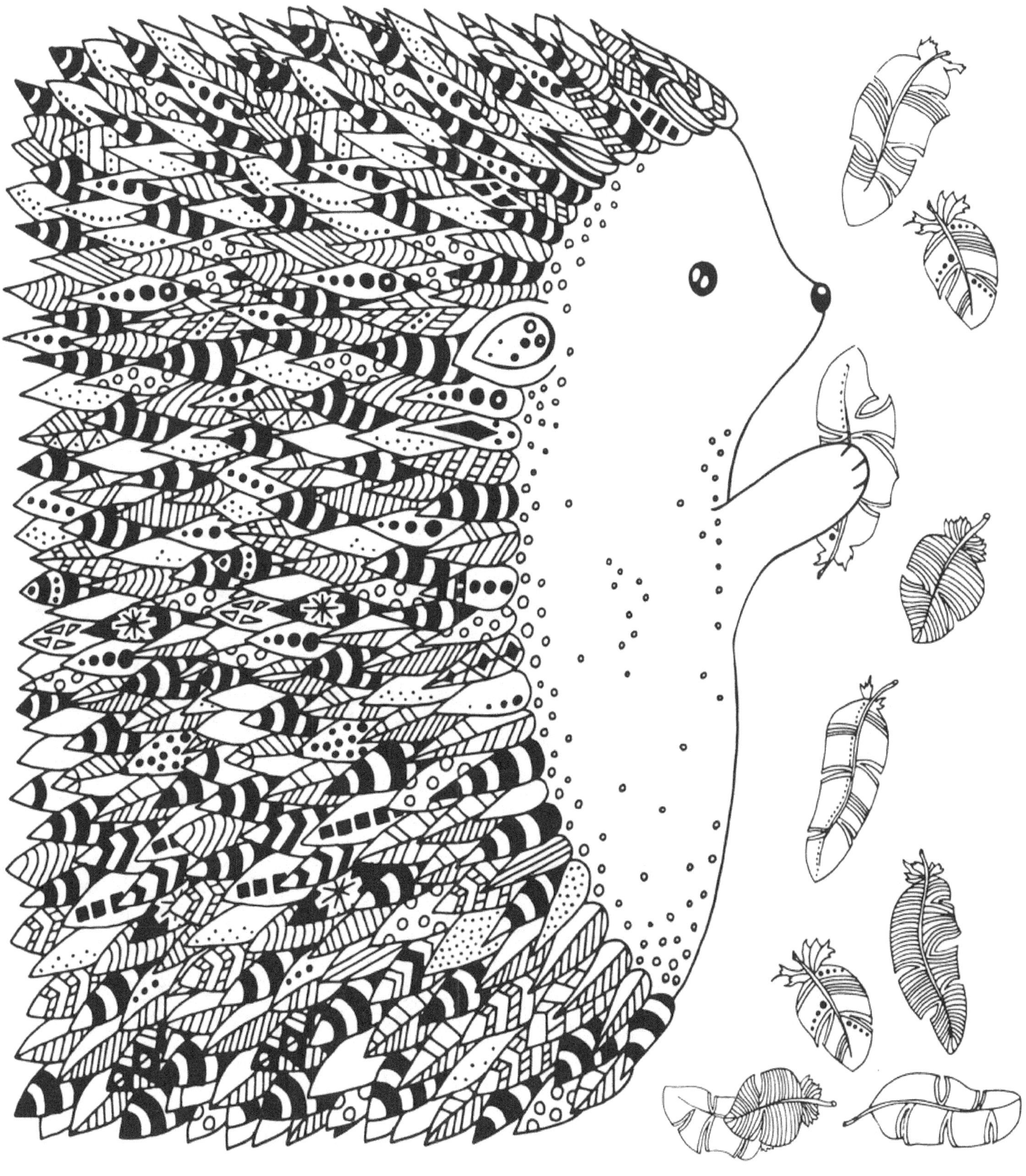

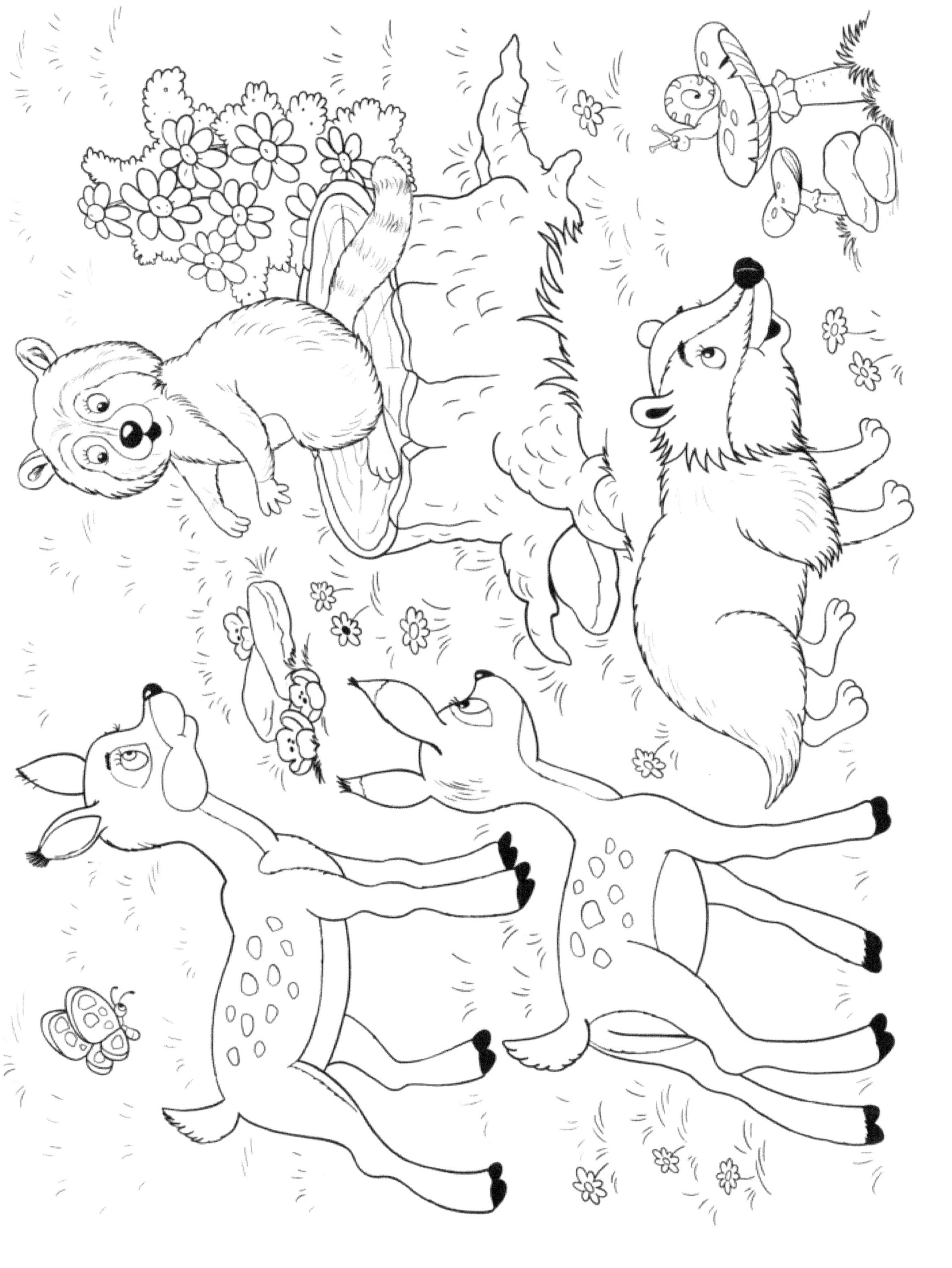

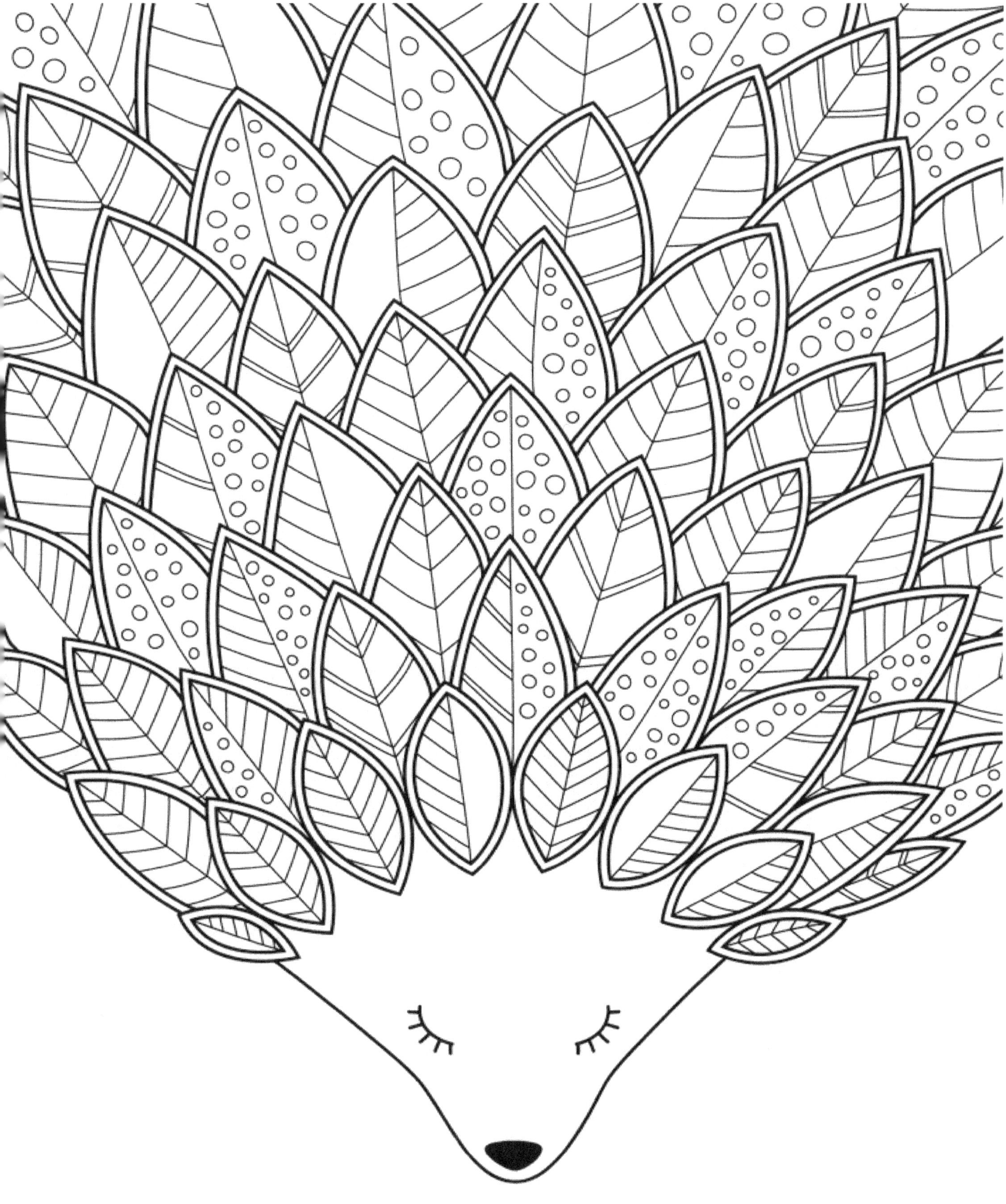

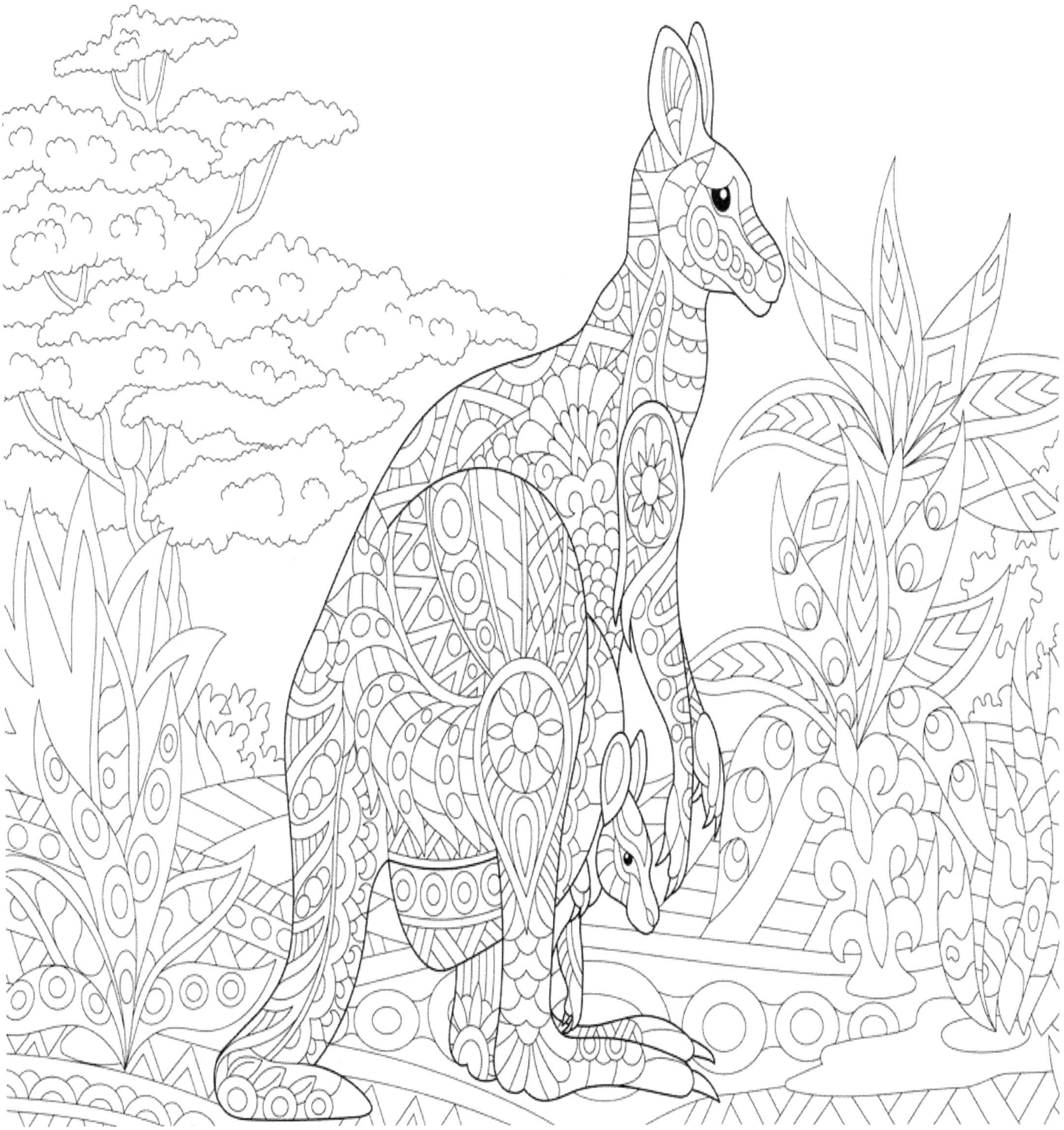

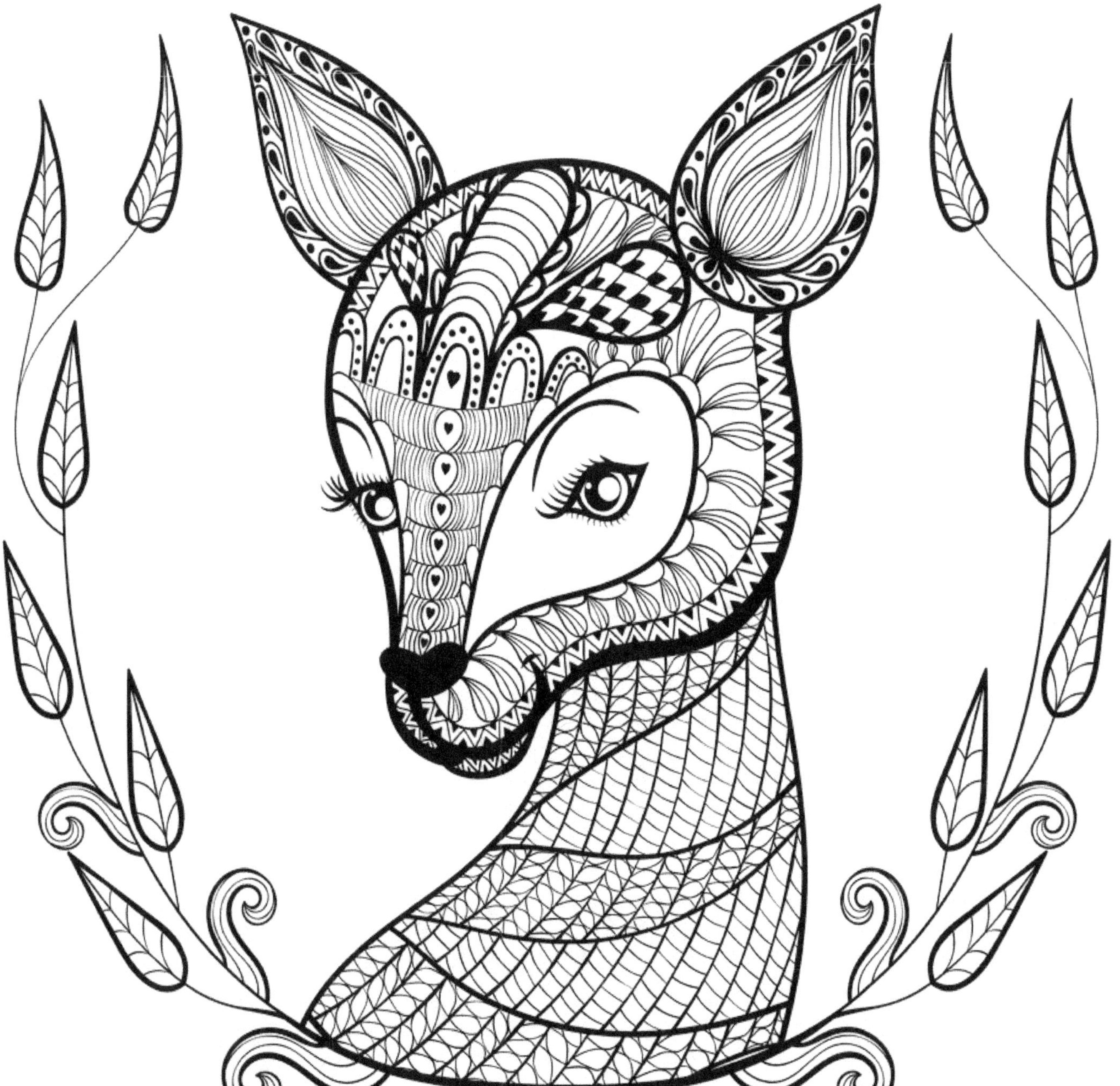

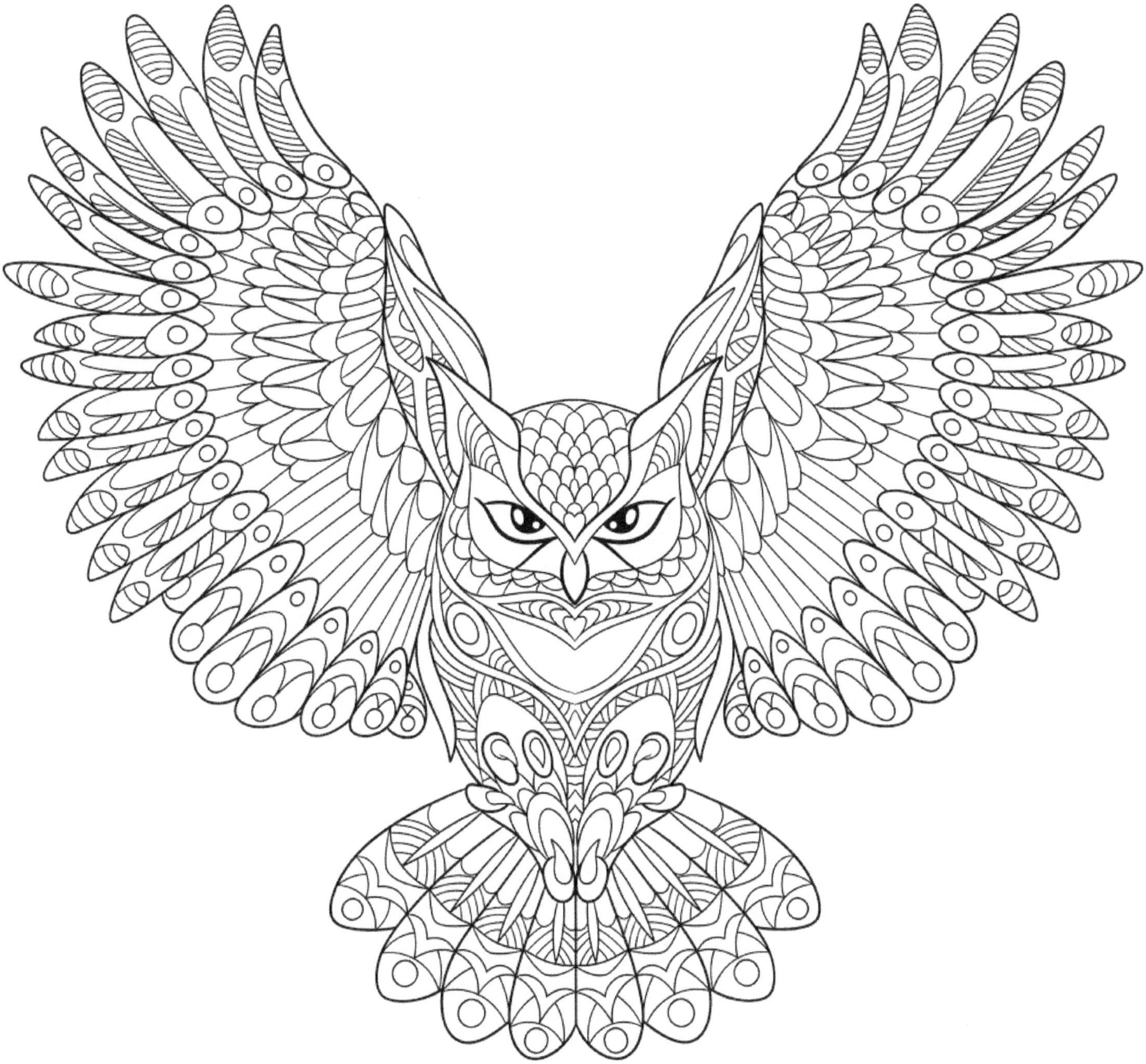

www.ingramcontent.com/pod-product-compliance
Lightning Source LLC
Chambersburg PA
CBHW082114220526
45472CB00009B/2177
9798682353163